THE ATLANTIS STORY

Why have the various attempts to 'find' Atlantis been unsuccessful?

For the good reason that Plato made the island up. Plato's Atlantis—the imperialist island state that disappeared in a cataclysm, leaving Athens to survive it—is just a myth.

Rather than focus on man's futile attempts to discover the island, Pierre Vidal-Naquet's brief history of Atlantis examines the diverse uses made of the myth through the ages in different contexts and periods. Written in a clear and interesting style, the depth of the author's knowledge is apparent in his deft use of primary references and the originality of his ideas is enhanced by carefully chosen illustrative material.

Pierre Vidal-Naquet was Director of Graduate Studies at the École des hautes études en sciences sociales in Paris until his death in 2006. He was one of the most famous French Classical scholars in the post-war period and has been widely translated. His earlier books in the field of Classics translated into English include: *Myth and Tragedy in Ancient Greece*; *The Black Hunter: Thought and Society in the Greek World*; *Economic and Social History of Ancient Greece*.

Janet Lloyd is one of the best known translators into English of French studies of the Classics; her many translations include *Plato and the City*, by Jean-François Pradeau, for University of Exeter Press.

THE ATLANTIS STORY

A SHORT HISTORY
OF PLATO'S MYTH

Pierre Vidal-Naquet

translated by Janet Lloyd

UNIVERSITY
of
EXETER
PRESS

First published in 2005 as *L'Atlantide: Petite histoire d'un mythe platonicien*
by Société d'édition Les Belles Lettres, Paris.

English language translation © University of Exeter Press 2007

English language translation
published in 2007 by
University of Exeter Press
Reed Hall, Streatham Drive
Exeter EX4 4QR
UK

www.exeterpress.co.uk

British Library Cataloguing in Publication Data
A catalogue record for this book is available
from the British Library.

ISBN 978 0 85989 805 8

Ouvrage publié avec le concours du Ministère français chargé de la culture—
Centre national du livre.

This book is supported by the French Ministry of Foreign Affairs, as part of the
Burgess programme run by the Cultural Department of the French Embassy in
London (www.frenchbooknews.com).

Liberté • Égalité • Fraternité
RÉPUBLIQUE FRANÇAISE

Typeset in Chaparral Pro 11pt on 15pt
by Carnegie Book Production, Lancaster
Printed in Great Britain by Antony Rowe Ltd, Chippenham

FOR GENEVIÈVE

CONTENTS

ILLUSTRATIONS

FOREWORD

G.E.R. LLOYD

P lato's myth of Atlantis continues to fascinate everyone who reads
it, political theorists, philosophers, novelists, poets, filmmakers.
But as this brilliant new study by Pierre Vidal-Naquet shows, that
tells us more about ourselves, our fantasies and our capacity for self-
deception, than about any respect we may have for Plato or about
our ability to give his texts the close critical reading they deserve.
Plato first briefly mentions, in the *Timaeus*, the story of the great
empire in a vast continent 'larger than Africa and Asia together' that
invaded Europe and was repelled by the heroic ancient Athenians
before both they and Atlantis itself were engulfed by a flood. Then
in the *Critias* we have the full-dress (though incomplete) story of
both ancient civilisations and their war.

Plato's own purposes, in his account, are complex, but, one might
have thought, transparent enough. He uses it, in effect, to kill three
birds with one stone. First it enables him to praise an ancient—
mythical—Athens that corresponds, in many respects, with the ideal
state that he had described in the *Republic*. It was because their
political regime was so well-ordered and harmonious that they were
victorious. Secondly, in criticizing the autocratic regime of Atlantis,
he evidently expresses disapproval of the autocratic Persian empire
whose invasion of Greece had had to be repelled at the battles
of Marathon, Salamis and Plataea. Thirdly he uses the story to

criticize obliquely and sometimes not just obliquely the maritime imperialism of contemporary Athens, for the story of Atlantis is of a wealthy and prosperous state that, overconfident in its sea power, turned aggressor and invaded its neighbours, and this bears obvious similarities to the recent behaviour of the Athenians during the Peloponnesian war.

Plato goes into extraordinary detail concerning the geographical location and extent of Atlantis, the layout of the city and its hinterland, its political and religious institutions and its eventual demise. This comes after it lost its sense of unity and justice—when the Gods chose to punish it first by its defeat in the war with ancient Athens, then by engulfing it under the waves and mud that thereafter made the passage between the ancient continent and Europe impassable.

With all that detail to hand, some ancient and many more modern writers have asked whether Plato was indeed drawing on some folk memory of real events. The hunt was on to identify the *real* Atlantis behind the myth, and as Vidal-Naquet shows, the answers have been astonishing. Many have found Atlantis in the continent Columbus 'discovered', of course, but other candidates have been proposed in droves, Africa, bits of mainland Europe, even Sweden. Time and again, astonishingly, the image of the ancient Atlantis has been turned into a vision of some kind of paradise. The account of its wealth is retained, but that of its aggression and injustice suppressed. Myth-making, as the anthropologists have taught us, is always a complex, multi-motivated activity of the human and social imagination. What is extraordinary about the way Plato's myth of Atlantis has been used, is that this has depended not on the re-telling of an oral tradition, but on the appropriation, manipulation and distortion of highly polished texts by often highly literate individuals. But while all the varying solutions on offer protest implicitly or explicitly that they do a better job than their rivals of meeting the geophysical specifications present in Plato's texts, none realizes, let alone admits,

that there *is* no single definitive solution that meets *all* those specifications—one that can provide a historical and geographical correlate
to the mythical picture that Plato presents. None stops to reflect that
Plato's purpose was *not* pseudo-history, *but* political analysis.

The great originality of this study is to focus not on any possible
historical basis for Atlantis, but on how the myth itself has run
riot in the hands of those who refuse to allow it to be just that,
a *myth*. The author, Pierre Vidal-Naquet, who corrected the final
version of this translation just before his tragic, premature, death,
in the summer of 2006, was one of the foremost intellectuals of
his generation. Along with his great friend, mentor and colleague,
Jean-Pierre Vernant, he transformed our understanding of ancient
Greek society and culture, not least in the great series of studies that
they published together, under the title *Myth and Tragedy in ancient
Greece*. Vidal-Naquet's *Black Hunter* combined historical analysis of
an Athenian initiatory institution with an exploration of a key
theme that runs through Greek literature of all types, that of the
passage from adolescence to adulthood, and that of the challenges to
character, determination and loyalty that that involves. In a series of
further studies, Vidal-Naquet shed light on the images and realities
of democracies, ancient and modern, and on the use made of ancient
models and ideals in the French and other modern revolutions, and
in yet others on the changing patterns of historiography in ancient
and early modern times.

But Pierre Vidal-Naquet was no mere academic intellectual, but an
engaged political activist. His very first book, before he had made
himself a stellar reputation as an ancient historian, was an exposé of
the cover-up of the murder, by the French authorities in Algiers, of
a dissident whom those authorities claimed 'disappeared' from police
custody. Over and over again Vidal-Naquet subsequently worked
tirelessly to expose lies and injustices, torture used in the name
of democracy, for instance, putting the record straight, including
refuting those who had denied the holocaust. His own father and

mother died in the concentration camps: that story and many other moving episodes are recounted in the two volumes of his *Mémoires*, an extraordinary document of an extraordinary life.

So Pierre Vidal-Naquet was responsible for many weightier and more influential tomes than this book. But the story of Atlantis remains a gem. It takes a mind as acute as his to shift the focus from the will o' the wisp of the 'real' Atlantis to the real subject of interest, namely what the obsession with that will o' the wisp can teach us about the vagaries and weaknesses of the human imagination.

Postscript from University of Exeter Press

For those who want to learn for themselves about the myth whose afterlife Vidal-Naquet recounts with such brilliance, there will soon be a new resource, also published by the University of Exeter Press. Christopher Gill, who has worked for some years on this topic, is preparing a book designed to bring together the materials for studying in depth the real Platonic Atlantis, rather than the products of modern fantasy. His book will include the Greek text of the Platonic account of Atlantis (the start of the Timaeus *and the fragmentary* Critias*), together with a new translation specially prepared for this publication. It will also include a full introductory essay, with an interpretative reading of the myth in the light of recent scholarship, as well as a commentary and vocabulary based on the Greek texts. This book is based on an earlier edition published originally in 1980; but the translation and introduction will be new and the commentary revised for this version. The combination of Vidal-Naquet's revelatory study of the reception of Plato's myth and Gill's edition of the real story will enable modern readers to regain access to a text which remains one of compelling interest.*

Preface to the
English Edition

For Ji and Geoffrey Lloyd

The French version of this little book was eventually published
in January 2005. One month later Editions Michel Houdiard
published the proceedings, edited by Chantal Fourcrier and Lauric
Guillard, of a colloquium held at Cérisy-la-Salle, in Normandy,
between 20 and 30 July 2002. I had been invited to that colloquium
but had been unable to attend it. Its organizers invited me to write
a preface to its *Atlantides imaginaires* (Imaginary Atlantises).[1] By
the time the present work appears in England, Italy and possibly
elsewhere too, fifty years will have passed since I began to take an
interest in Atlantis.

The point at which I began to do so was a lecture that I
attended in Orleans, when I was working there, in 1955–56, as
a young teacher in a secondary school for boys. The speaker was
an illustrious Sorbonne professor, Fernand Robert. He suggested,
although not too emphatically, that Plato might have been inspired
by the Minoan civilization. I myself did not see quite how, eight
long centuries after its disappearance, he could possibly have known
about it. My only authority to pronounce on this matter stemmed
from a *diplôme d'études supérieures* (a diploma of advanced studies)
on La conception platonicienne de l'histoire (Plato's conception of

history) on which I had been examined in October 1953 by Henri-Irénée Marrou. In the course of writing that thesis, I had become convinced not only that Plato was no historian (by no means an astounding discovery), but furthermore that in his seemingly historical texts, that is to say the *Laws*, the prologue to the *Timaeus*, the *Critias* and the *Republic*, he manifested a pronounced hostility toward history as practised by Herodotus and Thucydides. When Plato wrote history, he engaged in pastiches rather than any direct enquiry. As Marrou pointed out, I had treated Plato as a philosopher rather than a historian.

My contacts with Italy and Italian researchers were at that time very limited. I was familiar only with Adolfo Levi's works on Plato's conception of time. But soon after the Orleans episode and with the support of André Aymard, who at that time played a leading role in ancient history, I was appointed as an assistant lecturer in the Faculty of Letters of Caen University. The Chair of Ancient History there was at that time occupied by Henri Van Effenterre, who had written a book on La Crète et le monde grec de Platon à Polybe (Crete and the Greek world from Plato to Polybius).[2] When I told him that I had read his thesis, I suspect he imagined that I was simply flattering him. We certainly did not approach Plato from the same angle, but despite our disagreements we remained friendly enough for him to realize that I was no flatterer. In 1963 he arranged an opportunity for me to visit the excavations at Mallia. However, this had no bearing on the subject of Atlantis.

The purpose of my work on that subject was not so much to write a thesis on Greek fourth-century historiography, which is what André Aymard had suggested, but rather to understand the significance, in Plato's thought, of the opposition between on the one hand the prehistoric Athens (taken by German historiographers to be the real early Athens), described to Solon by the priest in Saïs, and, on the other, Atlantis, the imperialist and maritime power that disappeared in a cataclysm while a purged Athens survived it. In short, my view was that the war between Athens and Atlantis was really a war between Athens and Athens.

I returned to the subject time and again, in particular in Pisa, to which I was invited in the 1970s by Giuseppe Nenci and then again, in 1979, by Arnaldo Momigliano, my teacher and, in truth, the master and teacher in everything to do with the history of historiography. It was at this point that I produced an essay entitled 'Hérodote et l'Atlantide: entre les Grecs et les Juifs. Réflexions sur l'historiographie du siècle des Lumières' (Herodotus and Atlantis: in between the Greeks and the Jews. Reflections on the historiography of the Age of Enlightenment).[3] In it I elaborated the idea (reproduced in the present volume) that when, in what became the Roman Empire, the Bible progressively became the major sourcebook, this entailed a number of unfortunate consequences for the historiography of certain nations. Conversely, when nations wished to write their own respective histories, for several of them (in particular sixteenth-century Spain and late seventeenth-century Sweden), Atlantis offered a means to share in or even replace the elect status of Israel. As will be seen, that was a choice made by a considerable fraction of German nationalists, including during the Hitlerian period. At that time, to be descended from the people of Atlantis meant not being descended from the Jews either spiritually or 'by blood'.

Italy too played a part in what I have proposed calling Atlanto-nationalism. Its principal hero was certainly Count Gian Rinaldo Carli, a native of Capodistria, now an Italian-speaking town that is part of Slovenia. Carli presented Italy as the heir to the most ancient of cultures, not by virtue of any Graeco-Roman legacy but as the result of the American influence transmitted by the people of Atlantis, which he located, suitably enough, in between Europe and America. I have commented briefly on this important figure, the author of *Lettere americane* (American Letters) (1770–81) that were translated into French. I could have said considerably more had I known of the excellent book that my colleague Marco Ciardi published in Bologna in 2002 and which he was kind enough to send me when he learnt of my own work.[4] I shall have occasion to return to this splendid work—and not solely on account of the figure of Count Carli. My earlier ignorance of it was the cause of a major lacuna that I now hope to repair (although, of course, others still remain). Apart from the very special cases of Jules Verne and Pierre Benoit, I set on one side the vast body of Romantic literature that flooded Europe in the nineteenth and twentieth centuries. To refer the reader to Chantal Foucrier's *Le Mythe littéraire de l'Atlantide*[5] seemed and still seems to me to be a perfectly adequate solution. For those anxious to know more, I should also indicate the very full collection of papers edited by Lauric Guillot in 2000.[6] it contains samples of both excellent and lamentable work. I imagine that similar collections are to be found in Italy.

The fact remains that manifestations of a passionate desire to locate Atlantis and the no less dotty quest for origins continue. Here is one tiny example. In 1985, Adalberto Giovannini, a professor at the University of Geneva, produced a hypothesis which, he reckoned, would solve the puzzle of Atlantis: might not Plato have been inspired by the disasters that befell Helike and Boura, in Achaea, on the north-west coast of the Peloponnese, where both cities were swallowed up by an earthquake in the winter of 373/372?[7] This idea explains nothing in Plato's text and there are, in any case, other similar examples, such as the flood that Thucydides mentions at III, 89, 3, at the Locrian Atalanta during the Peloponnesian War.

Nevertheless, in a colloquium held from 11 to 13 July that same year,[8] in Melos, home to a famous statue of Aphrodite, an Achaean archaeologist, Dora Katsonopolou, announced the creation of a Helike Project designed to develop this 'illuminating comparison'. This was a very strange colloquium. It did, admittedly produce one or two reasonable suggestions,[9] but also some really mad ones. For example, three of its participants collaborated in trying to explain the concentric structure of the capital of Atlantis: just as a stone tossed into water produces the appearance of concentric rings, a meteorite from space could have created concentric circles in some unspecified location of this type.[10] And there was inevitably one scholar present, Jaime Manuschevich of the University of Chile, who was determined yet again to unearth the old hypothesis that 'Atlantis was Israel'.

Meanwhile the Internet has announced the forthcoming appearance of a dissertation by Nguepe Taba II of the J.W. Goethe University in Frankfurt, entitled *Afrika als Atlantis Insel*. The author claims that this myth that Solon borrowed from the Egyptian sages was both a reality—Atlantis truly was Africa—and also the result of a transformation designed 'to serve as the basis for colonial action on the part of the Greeks'; it also serves as a modern expression of European colonial ideology. The elements of truth present in this idea have been impeccably analysed by the late lamented G. Gliozzi, whom I have cited abundantly in the present book. All the rest is pure verbiage.

In concluding this Preface, allow me to return to the book by Marco Ciardi, *Atlantide. Una controversia scientifica da Colombo a Darwin*, primarily in order to emphasize its great merits. As I have mentioned above in connection with Carli, had I known of this work before writing my own (as was chronologically possible), I might have written a different book. Marco Ciardi provides many insights into a whole series of problems, in particular relating to Hooke and Stensen, the seventeenth-century earth-scientists to whom Alain Schnapp had drawn my attention but whom I have hardly mentioned, and the biblical writings of Newton, which I did mention but only very briefly. Furthermore, he makes many useful comments on Buffon, Spallanzani and Le Chevalier, showing how the latter two eighteenth-century scholars linked the quest for Atlantis with research concerned with Troy, a subject upon which I have barely touched; and he provides crucial information on Cuvier, Humboldt and Darwin, about whom I have said nothing at all.

In the first place, our respective objectives differed. What I set out to study in this book, as its sub-title indicates, is the history of a myth. Marco Ciardi, for his part, writes the history of a scientific controversy in which a number of real intellectuals took part (not all, however: Descartes, a philosopher and mathematician if ever there was one, had nothing at all to say about Atlantis). On the other hand, what about Montaigne, to whom Ciardi devotes a few lines: does he really earn a place in the history of a scientific quarrel? Moreover, is it possible to identify a single concept of 'science' that is common to both Christopher Columbus and Darwin? That of mathematics, perhaps? Pierre de Fermat (1601–65) was the author of a theorem that he claimed (in a marginal note to an edition of the Greek mathematician Diophantus) to have proved. While travelling in Greece in 1993, in the company of Spyros Spathis and Laurent Schwartz, both mathematicians, I learnt that the theorem had eventually been proved once and for all only under circumstances that suggested that it was unlikely that Fermat had really hit upon the solution.[11] Fermat was a member of the provincial government of Toulouse. Professionally, he was a jurist. In mathematics he was, as the saying went, the 'prince of amateurs'.

The professionalization of knowledge was a long drawn-out process, even for the exact sciences. There was not just one scientific revolution, but several, a whole succession of 'paradigms', to borrow Thomas S. Kuhn's expression,[12] or 'epistemological fields', as Michel Foucault would have said.

In the controversy surrounding Atlantis, as studied by Marco Ciardi, what makes things horribly complicated is the fact that it was treated as though it was a matter of a geographical or geological problem combined, however, with a biblical tradition that weighed heavily upon it, even in the nineteenth century.

Was scepticism such as that evinced by Voltaire a sufficient antidote to this kind of credulousness?[13] What makes the story of Atlantis such a striking and special case is that one needs to remove it from the real world (which did not happen until the 1841 *Dissertation* produced by Thomas-Henri Martin, who was a truly professional historian of ancient philosophy and science) and at the same time to interpret it as Plato himself conceived it, that is to say as a radical critique of the maritime imperialism of Athens. This interpretation, which I have endeavoured to resuscitate, was proposed for the first time by Giuseppe Bartoli, who was born in 1717 and taught Italian oratory and Greek literature at the University of Turin from 1745 to 1763. In 1779, he published his crucial work, *An Essay on Plato's own historical explanation of his Atlantis, which has so far not been taken into consideration.* Bartoli's book was widely misunderstood, even by Thomas-Henri Martin.[14]

Unlike Voltaire, Georges Cuvier (1769–1832) believed in the existence of fossils, but ruled out human ones. He thought that the earth's history had repeatedly been punctuated by catastrophes and that the merit of Plato's 'poetic imagination' was that it took us back to the major crisis of the Flood and the Bible.[15]

The transition from a geologist's Atlantis to the Atlantis of poets and novelists thus proceeded extremely slowly. As will be seen, in the present book I use the name of Jules Verne to symbolize that second phase. However, as will also be seen, as early as 1797, Fabre d'Olivet (1767–1825), the 'imperial theosophist', was already beginning to speculate about the people of Atlantis. The same can be said of German Romantics such as Novalis, who idealized what, for Plato, was an empire of evil, and turned it into a secret paradise.

The great scholar Alexander von Humboldt, who was born in Berlin in 1769 and died in 1859, arrived in Paris in 1798. Between 1799 and 1804 he was exploring South America and raising questions about the geography of Atlantis without, it seems to me, adopting any definite position on the matter. As a German who chose to write in French, he was, of course, utterly unaffected by any kind of Atlanto-nationalism.[16]

I am also grateful to Marco Ciardi for the information that Charles Darwin, the author of *On the Origin of Species* (1859), under the influence of, among others, the botanist J.D. Hooker, reverted to the hypothesis of a lost continent to which the Atlantic islands testified since they constituted the tips of its highest mountains. This only goes to show that science most definitely neither progresses consistently forward nor speaks with a single voice.

Fayence, July 2005

ACKNOWLEDGEMENTS

This little book could not have been written without the help of many of my close friends: Jacques Brunschwig, who initiated me into the *Timaeus* many decades ago, and who has read and reread this book as closely as if it were his own; Michel Desgranges, who asked me to write this book and has supported me throughout; Arno J. Mayer, who used the immense resources of the library of Princeton on my behalf; Maud Sissung, who transformed my manuscript into a viable book, a task that, as always, she fulfilled to perfection; Chantal Foucrier, my sister in Atlantology; Hervé Duchêne, Jesper Svenbro, Marie-Laurence Descolos, Gilles Dorival, Jean-Christophe Saladin, Luc Brisson, Yvon Garlan, Riccardo Di Donato, Charalampos Orfanos, Ingrid Galster, Charles Malamoud, Yves Touchefeu, Denise Fourgous, François Lissarrague, Adrian Le Bihan, Claude Lefort, Carlos Miralles, and in particular Alain Schnapp, who provided me with many documents, and Nicole Sels, who always responded to my demands. I should also like to thank Agnès Tapin, the archivist at the Centre Louis Gernet, and Jean-François Bassinet, in the production department of Les Belles Lettres, who worked hard to produce a satisfactory result. My thoughts also go to my deceased friend Simon Pembroke who, many years ago now, sent me one of the books upon which this study is founded.

TRANSLATOR'S NOTE

I have used the following English translations of Classical authors, in the Loeb Classical Library.

Aristotle
De Caelo, trans. by W.K.C. Guthrie, 1945
Meteorologica, trans. by H.D.P. Lee, 1962

Dionysius of Halicarnassus
Letter to Pompey, trans. by Stephen Usher, 1961

Herodotus
Histories, trans. by A.D. Godley, 1946

Lucian
A True Story, trans. by A.M. Harmon, 1979

Philo of Alexandria
De Aeternitate Mundi, trans. by F.H. Colson, 1941

Plato
Critias, Menexenus, Timaeus, trans. by R.G. Bury, 1926
Laws, trans. by R.G. Bury, 1926
Republic, trans. by Paul Shorey, 1946

Tertullian
Apology, trans. by T.R. Glover, 1966

INTRODUCTION

This little book has been germinating within me for almost half a century. In 1953, in the presence of Henri-Irénée Marrou, I defended a 'diploma of advanced studies' (today it would be called a 'master's dissertation') on The Platonic Conception of History. It was, in truth, the work of a historian of philosophy rather than history in the traditional sense of the word. In this thesis, which afforded me my first chance to read the entire works of Plato, a few pages were devoted to Atlantis. Six years later, in 1959, Raymond Weil published his *Archéologie de Platon*, in which he raised the question of the sources of Plato's 'historical' stories, in particular that told in *Laws*, book III, and concluded that it was a kind of pastiche of history as practised by the great Greek historians, Herodotus and Thucydides.

As a young teacher at the Lycée Pothier, in Orleans, from 1955 to 1956, I attended a lecture by Fernand Robert, professor of Greek at the Sorbonne. In this he presented the 'Cretan hypothesis' but (to his credit) did so somewhat hesitantly: was it the case that the civilization of Atlantis, in which the sacrifice of bulls was prominent and which was so luxurious and boasted such splendid monumental architecture, must owe something to the splendours of the Minoans? One immediate objection sprang to mind. How could Plato have known about a Cretan culture that had vanished a thousand years earlier? True, Thucydides had declared Minos to be the first inventor of a thalassocracy; however, he had—with good reason—said nothing about the wealth of the sovereigns of Cnossus or about gold or, again with good reason, about the unknown metal, orichalcum. My own feeling was that, contrary to Thucydides's opinion, the Minoan thalassocracy owed much to the Athenian one, as developed after and even during the Persian Wars.

Atlantis too was a thalassocracy. Its origins went back to Poseidon's love for the nymph Clito. Clito presented the god with five pairs of twins and these became the first ten kings of Atlantis. Its terrestrial and maritime space had been divided without strife (*ou kat'erin*) between the gods for, as Plato explains, 'it would not be reasonable to suppose that the gods were ignorant of their own several rights, nor yet that they attempted to acquire for themselves, by means of strife, a possession to which others, as they knew, had a better claim'.[1]

Those words show that Plato was critical of the Athenian tradition, with which he was certainly familiar since it was illustrated on the west pediment of the Parthenon, sculpted by Phidias and Ictinus, and he himself pokes fun at it in the pastiche of a funeral speech included in the *Menexenus*: 'Our country is deserving of praise, not only from us but from all men, on many grounds, but first and foremost because she is god-beloved. The strife (*eris*) of the gods who contended over her and their judgement (*krisis*) testify to the truth of our statement.'[2]

In the divine distribution mentioned in the *Critias*, what really interested Plato was Athens, which was dominated partly by Athena and Hephaestus, the deities of wisdom and craftsmanship respectively, and partly by Poseidon, the 'earth-shaker' of the Homeric world and above all, the god of the sea. Although that division was effected 'without strife', both the prologue to the *Timaeus* and the *Critias* nevertheless refer to the battle between 'the children of Athena', as Nicole Loraux calls them, and the descendants of Poseidon, every one of these a thalassocrat if ever there was one.

While these ideas were taking shape in my mind, I was making new intellectual acquaintances: first and foremost Pierre Lévêque, the late and much lamented archaeologist and historian of Greece, also

Jean Bollack and Heinz Wismann who, together, had founded in Lille a centre of studies in Greek thought that I have sometimes likened to the monastery of the Sleepless in Constantinople. The Sleepless were, as their name suggests, those who never slept because, in their monastery, a prayer was supposed to rise up to heaven at every hour of the day and the night.

My collaboration with Lévêque produced a book, *Cleisthenes the Athenian*,[3] in which we first sketched in the rivalry between, on the one hand, a democratic and imperialistic Athens that Plato did not much like and, on the other, the Athens presented as an ideal in the *Republic* and elaborated as far as was practically possible in the *Laws*. That rivalry constitutes the basis of my own interpretation of the Atlantis of the *Timaeus* and the *Critias*. Of course, I could see that the Atlantis of the *Critias* was not exactly democratic. But as Chapter 1 of the present work will attempt to show, in the eyes of Plato the Athenian democracy and the Persian Empire constituted two models that were equally threatened by degeneration.

Right or wrong, my interpretation was the subject of a paper written for 'L'Association pour l'encouragement des études grecques' (The Society for the Promotion of Hellenic Studies), which was published first in the 1964 *Revue des études grecques* and later in my book entitled *The Black Hunter*.[4] It goes without saying that this interpretation radically excluded any possibility that Atlantis had ever existed as an island and a political power in the ocean that still reminds us of its name. At this point Georges Dumézil wrote to wish me 'the very best of luck with the Hellenists'.

Other analyses were now appearing, some of which took my remarks into account, others that ignored them. In particular, Christopher Gill, in Wales, produced a study in which he referred explicitly to my analysis,[5] as did J.V. Luce, in Ireland.[6] Those who took part in my seminar at the École des Hautes Études added many useful contributions and further developed some of my hypotheses.[7] Two scholars who were particularly helpful were Jesper Svenbro, who brought to my attention the Gothic-tinged ideology of Olof Rudbeck, and Marie-Laurence Desclos.[8]

In the course of these discussions I sometimes crossed swords with Luc Brisson, a stolid Québequois to whom I was sometimes obliged to surrender my weapons.[9] Subsequently we met on several occasions, serving as co-examiners of the doctoral theses of scholars such as Marie-Laurence Desclos and Anissa Castel Bouchouchi, who produced a major essay comparing ideas on the Platonic corpus as her contribution to a colloquium in Cérisy.[10]

Among the works that I encouraged, without actually meeting their authors, was the important book by Jean-François Pradeau, *Le Monde de la politique. Sur le récit atlante de Platon*.[11] Pradeau diverges from my ideas only on points of a very secondary nature while, for my part, it is mainly the title of his book that leaves me hesitant. I myself would prefer to speak of an anti-political world, for—with the exception of warfare—Plato condemns all the activities of an Athenian citizen.[12] The primitive Athens of the prologue to the *Timaeus* and the *Critias* encourages warrior activities and is governed by gods, not by itself nor by human politicians.

Quite apart from my pleasure at being cited, how could I not rejoice when I read, in Richard Ellis's excellent *Imagining Atlantis*: 'Is it not possible to believe that Plato wrote the story of Atlantis as a parable of the demise of Pericles' Athens?'[13] In contrast, how not to smile—or indeed weep—upon reading, in a 'serious' work that itself refers to a 'serious' journal, that Plato misread the notes written by Solon, who had declared that the island of Atlantis was half-way (*meson*) between Libya and Asia, not that it was larger (*meizōn*) than the two put together? This 'serious' author then herself proceeded to indulge in a little emendation of her own, solemnly explaining that in truth it was Solon who had misread the Egyptian sources![14] Alas, when realism gets a hold on us ....

In my opinion, two outstanding works now dominate the enquiry into the history of the myth of Atlantis. One is the huge thesis

1. The Standard of Ur (2500–2350 BC), © The Trustees of the British Museum. *See p. 11 and p. 115*

defended in 1996 by Chantal Foucrier, entitled *Le Mythe littéraire de l'Atlantide*,[15] of whose existence I learnt only in the spring of 2002. This thesis by and large takes my own works into account but, naturally enough, adopts a different approach: it studies the myth as it appears in literary works, whereas I reflected, rather, on the myth in history. That being said, we both seem to be pulling in the same direction.

The other work is the one that I mention, in connection with Jules Verne, in Chapter 6 of the present book: *The Atlantis Syndrome*, by the British historian and archaeologist Paul Jordan.[16] The term 'syndrome', borrowed from the vocabulary of medicine, is perfectly justified, for it refers to a recurrent indisposition. I wish I had written this book. There are, to be sure, a few lacunae in it. For example, it makes no mention of Cosmas Indicopleustes, the Byzantine author of whom I write in Chapter 2 of the present work; but then my own study also contains lacunae and it seems to me that we complement each other splendidly.

For my part, after studying Plato's text, I have applied myself to considering its successive interpretations in the course of ancient, modern and contemporary history.[17] The present volume presents the results of those studies. I start by comparing Atlantis—this piece of anti-history—with the various forms of nationalism that have succeeded one another in European and American history. Next, I embark upon a comparison between two myths, Plato's and the one that relates to the (true) story of Masada, according to Flavius Josephus's account. Lastly, the authors who gathered at the Cérisy colloquium in July 2002 kindly asked me to write a preface to their collected papers.

Despite my own best efforts and those of sceptical colleagues whose thinking runs along lines similar to mine, there has been no staunching the flow of 'realist' interpretations. Let me now mention just a few of them, obviously leaving aside those of a purely fraudulent or popularizing nature.

2. A ship entering a port. The Akrotiri (Santorini) fresco, sixteenth century BC, Athens, National Museum. *See p. 11*

Jacques Collina-Girard, a geologist from Aix-en-Provence, has forcefully suggested that Plato may have been inspired by an archipelago immersed in the last great ice age to the west of the straits of Gibraltar: an island 14 kilometres long and 5 kilometres wide, surrounded by a scattering of smaller islands: all of which fits perfectly well with Plato, provided you suppress all his indications as to the island's dimensions and its ostentatious wealth.[18] But were you to do that, you might just as well suggest locating Atlantis in the boating pond of the Jardin de Luxembourg.

A number of other solutions have been put forward, a few of which I discuss in the later chapters of this book. But let me now mention one or two others that have attracted a measure of interest.

Eberhard Zangger, a geo-archaeologist living in Zurich and associated with the Cambridge University Department of Earth Sciences, has published a book, *The Flood from Heaven*, prefaced and sanctioned by my excellent colleague and friend, the eminent archaeologist Anthony Snodgrass.[19]

Not everything is false in this well-written book. For example, it is quite true and has for a long time been known that the island of the Phaeacians described in the *Odyssey* bequeathed something to Plato's Atlantis. But there is no getting away from the fact that Plato lived several centuries later than Homer. The central idea of Zangger, who assimilates Atlantis to Troy, possesses a nugget of truth if the Homeric Troy about which Plato read in the *Iliad* is what is at issue, but it becomes absurd if Atlantis is to be compared to the historical and archaeological Troy that Schliemann, Dörpfeld and Blegen excavated at Hissarlik; for Plato, who was no archaeologist, could only have known of Troy through Homer.

It is one thing to note, as Zangger, following Christopher Gill, indeed does, that Plato's style is 'very historical',[20] But it is quite another to confuse a pastiche of Herodotus with Herodotus or Thucydides themselves.[21] Plato was a brilliant creator of pastiches, as he also shows in the *Menexenus* and the *Phaedrus*, but he was

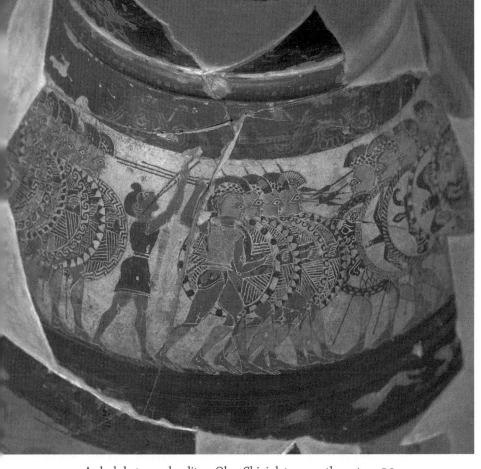

3. A clash between hoplites, Olpe Chigi, late seventh century BC
Rome; National Etruscan Museum of the Villa Giulia, Rome.

not a historian of reality. Trojan Atlantis is the creation of Zangger
alone. The trouble is that Troy was besieged and conquered by the
Achaeans and, as Peter James points out, 'an Atlantis that does not
sink beneath the waves is no Atlantis at all'.[22]

Two other hypotheses have largely dominated the field of
'scholarly' studies on the localization of the island in Plato's story.

One favours Minoan Crete, discovered by Arthur Evans in 1900 and since then excavated by the British, French, Italian, German and Greek schools of archaeology. In the summer of 1963, I was present at the excavations at Mallia, to which I had been invited by Henri Van Effenterre, whose assistant I had been in Caen. As far as I can remember, no one there even mentioned the theme of Atlantis (fortunately).

As it happens, the appearance of the Minoan hypothesis can be precisely dated. On 19 February 1909, an anonymous letter was published in *The Times* of London (see appendix, pp. 171–82). The author of that letter, K.T. Frost, made himself known a few years later, with a scholarly article.[23] He was then teaching at the University of Belfast. Frost was not alone in seeking—and finding—Atlantis in Greece. As the author of an article entitled 'Atlantis found again', which situated it in Lake Copaïs in Boeotia, disarmingly remarked, 'the major difficulty lies in the fact that Plato's Atlantis is located far to the west, whereas Lake Copaïs is in central Greece'.[24]

But that conjecture was no more than a flash in the pan. The other Greek hypothesis that has caused much ink to flow, much of it of a patriotic nature, locates Atlantis on the island of Santorini (Thera). This was supported in particular by the Greek archaeologist Spiridon Marinatos (1901–74) and also enthralled the French underwater explorer Jacques-Yves Cousteau.[25] The two hypotheses run together to the extent that, in the view of some scholars, it was the eruption of the Santorini volcano that caused the destruction of the Minoan civilization at a date that varies according to different archaeologists but must have been somewhere around the middle of the second millennium BC.[26]

As early as 1939, in the journal *Antiquity*, Marinatos set out the hypothesis that the Minoan civilization was destroyed in a huge eruption of the volcano of Santorini; and in 1950, he published in the Greek journal *Kritika Chronica* an article that was subsequently translated into English.[27] In this he suggested that Plato, after spending some time in Egypt, could have been inspired to write the Atlantis legend by the explosion on Santorini.

To be sure, his dating is different from of that of Plato, who places the event some 9,000 years before Solon, but in the domain of dating all kinds of liberties are permissible and possible. In 1967, Marinatos began excavations on the Akrotiri promontory of Santorini, where he continued to work right up to his death there, in 1974. He had discovered a magnificent city of the Minoan type, which was promptly dubbed the Bronze Age Pompeii.[28] Marinatos was a great patriot. However, despite the considerable masses of pumice-stone ejected for great distances (even as far as Palestine) by the Santorini volcano, I must confess that I do not believe that Plato's invention can be merged with the presence in Santorini of a town that Plato, miraculously, moved to the Atlantic Ocean.

And now, in default of finding Atlantis and having returned the myth that Plato created to Athens, let me try to sketch in its history. It is true that Athens boasts an 'Atlantis Museum' in an outlying quarter of the modern capital; but when I tried to visit it, in 2002, I was told that it was always closed.

Fayence, July 2003–September 2004

P.S. It would be possible to produce a picture book, larger than the present volume, with illustrations ranging from Greek art to modern strip-cartoons and including efforts at map-making. In the present volume, the illustrations that provide a modest counterpoint to the text, starting with the Ur standard, are simply intended to show that the theme of the two cities is far more ancient than the philosopher who invented Atlantis.

CHAPTER 1

IN THE BEGINNING WAS PLATO

_____

Why the above title for this first chapter? Because, before considering what people have made of Plato, it is important to understand what he himself actually said. I am well aware of a likely immediate objection: if it is today possible to understand what Plato *meant* to say in the prologue to the *Timaeus* (17a–27b) and in the *Critias*, which breaks off at the point where Zeus is about to propose before the assembly of the gods that the great island be destroyed, then all the rest of my story of the subsequent interpretations of his intentions becomes absurd. I myself obviously believe that to be nonsense: history is not made up solely of the triumphs of the human mind but also incorporates its mistakes and the many dead-ends into which it has blundered and continues to blunder.

In 1841, Thomas-Henri Martin, a disciple of Victor Cousin, published a long 'Dissertation on Atlantis'[1] in his famous *Studies on Plato's Timaeus*, which established the bases for a scholarly commentary on the most difficult dialogue written by the founder of the Academy. This dissertation passed in review all the hypotheses that scholars of varying repute had so far produced on the localization of the large vanished island. On the first page of his study and also on the last, Thomas-Henri Martin made his own view absolutely clear: 'As I see it, Atlantis belongs no more to the history of events than it does to real geography; however, unless I am very much mistaken, it may contribute a very intriguing chapter to the no less interesting and no less instructive history of human opinions.' In conclusion, he declared, 'Some have thought that they recognized Atlantis in the New World. No, it belongs to a different world, one to be found not in the spatial domain but in that of thought.' Nothing could be more true, and I have long been of the opinion that the history of all these ramblings should have been brought to a close at the point where Martin reached his conclusion. 'He was the first (but not the last) scholar who seems sober, after so many drunkards', as the contemporary philosopher Jacques Brunschwig, himself an excellent disciple of Aristotle, remarked to me, freely paraphrasing what Aristotle says about Anaxagoras in *Metaphysics* A 984b 15–18.

What we have before us are two dialogues, or rather two fragments. The *Timaeus* is an austere dialogue that contains an account of Plato's physics, relayed by Timaeus of Locris, a figure about whom all we really know is what Plato is prepared to tell us in the dialogue that bears his name:

> Our friend Timaeus is a native of a most well-governed State, Italian Locris, and inferior to none of its citizens either in property or in rank; and not only has he occupied the highest offices and posts of honour in his State, but he has also, in my opinion, attained the very summit of eminence in all branches of philosophy.[2]

The sources that present him as a Pythagorean are all later than Plato and are inspired by this dialogue. His historical existence is not proven but not improbable.

However, it is not Timaeus but Critias who tells the story that he says he has heard from his grandfather and namesake, Critias the Elder. This Critias, aged 90 at the time, attributed to Solon a story that the priests of Neith (the Egyptian name for Athena) told the Athenian lawgiver long, long ago. It is more or less pointless to try to establish a dramatic date for this dialogue. Hermocrates, who was to be the spokesman of a third dialogue (*Critias* 108a), was a Syracusan general who defeated the Athenians in 413 BC and left Syracuse when the Sicilian city became a democracy. Critias, Plato's cousin, was the most famous of the Thirty Tyrants who took over power in Athens after its defeat. He died a violent death in 403. Clearly then, this fictional dialogue is a dialogue of the dead whose protagonists in all likelihood never even met. Besides, Plato regularly took so many liberties with the history of Athens and Greece in general that it is pointless to seek to establish a likely dramatic date.

Most interpreters date the writing of the *Timaeus* and the *Critias* to around 355, that is to say following the collapse of the second Athenian Confederation. Athens was then governed by moderates the most significant of whom was Eubolus, and at this point it gave up the maritime imperialism that had contributed to its glory ever since the end of the Persian Wars. As we shall see, the themes fiercely debated in the *Timaeus* and the *Critias* themselves help to establish the dating of these two dialogues.

Have the texts come down to us complete? The question only arises in the case of the *Critias*: Pierre Benoit—and he alone—has drawn attention, in his *Atlantide*, to the presence in the Hoggar of a manuscript containing a full text of the *Critias*. But was it not Plato's own intention that the dialogue should remain unfinished? One perspicacious scholar has noted that, right from the start of the *Timaeus*, Plato alerts the reader to the incomplete nature of the situation. For what does Socrates say? 'One, two, three—but where, my dear Timaeus, is the fourth of our guests of yesterday?' And Timaeus replies, 'Some sickness has befallen him, Socrates; for he would never have stayed away from our gathering of his own free will.'[3]

But what exactly did take place the evening before, in the course of the philosophical symposium the conclusions of which Socrates summarizes here? It is usually claimed that Socrates is summing up the contents of the *Republic*. That is both true and false. It is true that all the same elements seem to be present: the Guardians' responsibility in the military domain, the prohibition of gold and silver, the equality between men and women, the community of women and children—everything except the idea of entrusting the city's leadership solely to philosophers. The exact wording in the *Republic* for the latter idea was: 'The soul of a guardian must be endowed with a particular nature. It must, as we said, be at once full of energy and tender toward philosophy.' But that notion is masked here: no distinction is made between a philosopher and a warrior. The conversation in the *Republic* began in the Piraeus (see Fig. 5, p. 31), at the time of the festival of the Bendidaea, devoted to a foreign deity, but it continued as the speakers made their way back to Athens. The discussion in the *Timaeus*, in contrast, takes place during Athens's major festival, the Panathenaea, to which reference is obliquely made (*Timaeus* 26e). By a very strange sleight of hand, Plato converts the normative analysis of the *Republic* into history, yet that work (the *Republic*) is itself then relegated to the world of myth: 'The city with its citizens which you described to us yesterday, as it were in a fable, we will now transport hither into the realm of fact (*epitalēthes*)' (*Timaeus* 26d).

With singular perversity, Plato proceeds to multiply the layers of what Roland Barthes (who was certainly familiar with the practice) called 'the effects of reality'. When, right at the end of the *Republic*, Socrates is about to describe the after-life, he says, 'It is not, let me tell you, ... the tale to Alcinous told that I shall unfold, but the tale of a warrior bold, Er, the son of Armenius, by race a Pamphilian.'[4] Yet nowhere more frequently than in the *Timaeus* does he repeat warnings of the type: 'This is no mere story.'[5]

Plato certainly begins by saying that the story that concerns Atlantis 'is derived from an ancient oral tradition' (*Timaeus* 20d); nevertheless, this story, 'though passing strange, is wholly true' (20d). The written sources of this tale are Egyptian (24a; 27b), but it is also transmitted orally and has thus been passed down from Solon to Critias the Elder, from him to his grandson Critias the Younger, then repeated by the latter first to Timaeus and Hermocrates, then in the presence of Socrates, and a third time, in more detail, in the dialogue that bears Critias's name. It is a story that has undergone a series of rememberings (26a). Yet, even as he insists that he is speaking the truth, Plato presents us with a fictitious Solon:

> If only he [Solon] had not taken up poetry as a by-play but had worked hard at it like others, and if he had completed the story he brought here from Egypt, instead of being obliged to lay it aside owing to the seditions and all the other evils he found here on his return,—why then, I say, neither Hesiod nor Homer nor any other poet would ever have proved more famous than he.
>
> (*Timaeus* 21c–d)

What better way of conveying that the Solon into whose mouth Plato puts his words is a fictitious figure and that the Athens that is described and that defeats Atlantis before the island is swallowed up by the sea that also sweeps away the land of Athens is simply a poetic fiction? The poem that Solon never wrote has been constructed by Plato and the story that Critias tells is based on notes written in Greek by Solon (*Critias* 113b) and preserved by Critias's family.

The fictional narrative is thus transmitted by three sets of figures. One of these is Egypt, or rather Egyptian priests who, in Plato, as in Herodotus, bear witness to the antiquity of the history of the human race. Herodotus (II, 142), already, believed that Egypt had survived a most curious phenomenon: 'Four times in this period, the sun rose contrary to his wont; twice he rose where he now sets, and twice he set where he now rises.' Only the country through which the Nile flows could testify to those changes. Plato's Egypt[6] is a repository of the antiquity of the world, but—paradoxically enough—it testifies that Athens is even more ancient than Egypt itself, for Athens had already existed for a thousand years when Saïs was founded (23e).

Only the Egyptians could testify that, nine thousand years before Solon, two antagonistic powers faced each other, Athens and Atlantis. The strength of Atlantis lay in the number of its soldiers, its maritime power and its imperial ambitions. Athens, meanwhile, relied on the excellence of its constitution and the valour of its twenty thousand hoplites. By some 'divine chance', what the Egyptian priests had told Solon was strangely similar to the *Republic* according to Socrates and Plato (*Timaeus* 25e, *Critias* 110c, ff.): 'As for the military class, which had been separated off at the commencement by divine heroes and dwelt apart, it was supplied with all that was required for its sustenance and training' (*Critias* 110c). At that time Athens was an immense acropolis, minutely described in the *Critias*,[7] that extended from the Gulf of Corinth to the land of Oropos. Athens was a spatial city, not at all the perfect city constructed in the *Republic*. On the contrary, it had more in common with the city of Magnesia that Plato was to construct in his last book, the *Laws*.[8]

The city described in the *Critias* was as unified as could be and as land-locked as could be imagined, with neither ports nor, clearly, a navy, in sharp contrast to the Athens that Plato knew, which presented the very image of 'the skeleton of a sick man' (*Critias* 111b). At the centre of the Acropolis stood the sanctuary of the founding gods, Hephaestus and Athena, who embodied respectively the love of craftsmanlike skills (*technē*) and the love of wisdom, in other words philosophy (*Critias* 109c). Around this stood the collective dwellings or barracks of the Guardians. Beyond these the artisans and peasants lived, all within this one precinct, 'as it were, the enclosure of a single dwelling' (*Critias* 112b). It all formed a single unit or unity; only one other element mattered: that of the male and female warriors, which had to be maintained at 'about twenty thousand'. There was a single spring that provided an inexhaustible flow of water (*Critias* 112d). Here the people lived and they and their children's children grew old, passing on their terrain and their institutions 'in succession, unaltered, to others like themselves' (*Critias* 112c). In this terrain 'they dwelt, acting as guardians of their own citizens and as leaders by their own consent of the rest of the Greeks' (*Critias* 112d–e). It is surely not exaggerated to suggest that this primitive Athens, as different as could be from the Athens ironically praised in the *Menexenus*, represents a political expression of 'the Same'. That is a theory that would certainly explain why the cosmology of the *Timaeus* is followed up by the *Critias*.[9] The primitive Athens is as far removed from history as could possibly be imagined.

Atlantis, in contrast, belongs to the world of history, as Plato understands this, apparently a world of pure 'Otherness'. In the *Timaeus* its description is sketched in and in the *Critias* it is carefully drawn in more detail. Even as I use that expression, 'the world of history', I realize that it will not really do, since for Plato all history was a pack of lies. The history of Atlantis traces an unrestricted development of Otherness. The *Timaeus* presents Atlantis at the height of its imperialistic activities, as an island that was 'larger than Libya and Asia put together' (*Timaeus* 24e), situated beyond the Pillars of Hercules (the straits of Gibraltar) in a 'real sea', not the 'frog-pond' mentioned in the *Phaedo*, which we know as the Mediterranean. Having vanquished Libya and northern Italy, Atlantis sets out to conquer Egypt, Greece and the rest of the Mediterranean world. Against it, Athens stands alone, as at Marathon, and it overcomes the invading forces and liberates the peoples that have been reduced to slavery. This pseudo-historical account raises a chronological difficulty that must surely be deliberate. Athens is 1,000 years older than Saïs, the Egyptian city founded by the goddess Neith (the Egyptian name for Athena) (*Timaeus* 23d–e). So how could the Egyptian hieroglyphs have preserved the description and story of the founding of the primitive Athens? Here, we clearly find ourselves deep in myth.

The myth starts with this huge island ruled by Poseidon, the god of the sea and the shaker of the earth, while Athena and Hephaestus rule over Athens. The dispute between Athena and Poseidon was a classic topos of Athenian mythology that was depicted on the western pediment of the Parthenon. However, no mention of it is made in the *Critias*. The apportioning of privileges was effected 'without strife' (*Critias* 109b). It would not have been seemly to imagine such wrangling among deities who, in Plato's view, could not be other than good.

All the same, at the origin of the Atlantis story lies Poseidon's desire (*epithumia*) for a girl, Clito, whose name evokes glory (*kleos*). Clito is the only daughter of an autochthonous couple 'born from the earth', just as the Athenians claimed to be. The names of Clito's parents are Evenor and Leukippe. Etymologically, Evenor evokes a man of valour, while the name Leukippe evokes the white horse which, in the mythical team of horses of the *Phaedrus*, symbolizes noble passion, *thumos* (while *epithumia*, desire, is represented by a black horse). Right from the start, there is thus a mixture, an intermingling of the divine and the human. And it is precisely the progressive predominance of the human element over the divine that, at the end of the *Critias*, brings about the degeneration of Atlantis and its people, who have become 'filled ... with lawless ambition and power', and that leads to Zeus's decision to destroy Atlantis.

Between the beginning and the end of Atlantis a long story unfolds, one that is a total fabrication by Plato, and that, unlike the story of primitive Athens, is stuffed full of numbers.[10]

In archaic Athens there are individuals, legendary kings, who—as if by chance—are involved in certain myths relating to Poseidon. One example is Erechtheus, who has slain three of the sons of the god of the sea.[11] Plato makes no reference to this, but could surely assume that his readers would know of it. However, let us return to the love affair between Poseidon and Clito. Clito, an orphan but a nubile one, lives on a hill in the middle of the great island. Poseidon turns this island into a fortress: 'He made circular belts of sea and land enclosing one another alternately, some greater, some smaller, two being of land and three of sea, which he wrought as it were out the midst of the island, as if using a potter's wheel, so as to be impassable for man, for at that time neither ships nor sailing were as yet in existence' (*Critias* 113d–e). At once, an element of duality is introduced. Athens has a single spring; Atlantis has two, 'one flowing warm from its source, the other cold'. We are in a world of oppositions. Clito presents Poseidon with five pairs of male twins, whom the god raises. Each pair comprises an elder and a younger twin, and the eldest of them all is called Atlas: hence the name of both the island and the sea, the Atlantic Ocean. In traditional mythology, Atlas was the son of the Titan Iapetus and it was he who held up the world; but Plato portrays him as a totally different figure. It is not necessary to be particularly well informed about Plato's oral teaching to claim that at this point we are in the region of what Aristotle called 'the indefinite dyad of the great and the small', traces of which are also to be found in the *Parmenides* and the *Philebus*.[12] Albert Rivaud comments, 'The total absence of women in the royal lineage no doubt seems surprising. But no subsequent explanation for this remarkable deficiency is given.'[13]

The island is fabulously wealthy, its natural potential boundless: it is rich in agriculture, in mines, gold and the famous orichalcum, in animals both domesticated and wild, including elephants, 'the largest and the most voracious of beasts', and also in fruits, possibly even lemons. 'All this that hallowed island ... produced in marvellous beauty and endless abundance' (*Critias* 115a–b). This is the realm of the *apeiron*, the limitless.

This superabundance explains how it is that Atlantis, a negative Utopia if ever there was one, has over the centuries constantly been treated as a positive one, a kind of earthly paradise. Perhaps the best explanation is that provided by Jean-François Mattei:

> The fascination exerted over the years by the myth of Atlantis perhaps stems from its general specular structure which, through its profusion of images, reveals the impassable limits of myth and the ultimate silence of speech. In this sense, the Atlantis mirror appears right from the start as a mirror of death in which all the fantasies of subsequent Utopias will be reflected.[14]

There can certainly be no doubt that Otherness is at work in Atlantis. The labours undertaken by the ten dynasties that sprang from Poseidon and Clito's five pairs of twins link the central island with the external sea. The kings construct both canals and bridges that break through the initial isolation of Clito's island: 'They assembled every fifth year and then alternately every sixth year, giving equal honour to both the even and the odd' (*Critias* 119d). (According to the Pythagorean tradition that Plato here follows, the uneven numbers were considered good, the even bad.) Progress, or at least movement, characterized the artistic endeavours of the rulers of Atlantis: 'As each king received [his palace] from his predecessor, he added to its adornment and did all he could to surpass the king before him, until finally they made of it an abode amazing to behold for the magnitude and beauty of its workmanship' (*Critias* 115c–d). There were five precincts, each corresponding to one pair of twins (*Critias* 113e–114d). Thanks to the canals, they were all interlinked. There were three harbours and then a wall with 'numerous houses built on to it, set close together; while the seaway and the largest harbour were filled with ships and merchants coming from all quarters, which, by reason of their multitude caused clamour and tumult of every description and an unceasing din night and day' (*Critias* 117e).[15] The scene is quite the reverse of the austere, military acropolis of the fictional 'primitive Athens'.

The next question that arises is: what is the nature of Plato's tale? Is it history? It would be about as reasonable to regard it as such as to take Lucian's *True Histories* seriously just because that is the title that he gives to the account of his journey to the moon, even though he is frank enough to explain: 'Everything in my story is a more or less comical parody of one or another of the poets, historians and philosophers of old, who have written much that smacks of miracles and fables. I would cite them by name, were it not that you yourself will recognize them from your reading.'[16] Plato is not as frank as Lucian. But that is no reason for not endeavouring to decipher his intentions and allusions. Not that I think that this really involves a 'philosophy of history' in the strict sense of the expression.[17] Rather, it is a matter of a pastiche of history, as Christopher Gill has rightly detected.[18] In similar fashion, in the *Menexenus*, Plato has Aspasia produce a pastiche of the funeral oration that Thucydides ascribes to Pericles after the first year of war and that Nicole Loraux has analysed so brilliantly in her *The Invention of Athens*. All of this goes to show that Plato had read Thucydides very closely indeed, just as he studied Herodotus attentively before proceeding to pastiche and criticize him. That is a point that I made way back in 1964, when I compared 'the great and marvellous exploits' of Athens mentioned by the *Timaeus* (20e) to the 'great and marvellous deeds done by Greeks and foreigners' that are evoked in the very first sentence of Herodotus's *Histories*. Since then, the point has been further developed in particular by Jean-François Pradeau, who has produced a close analysis of the 'Herodotean lexicon of the *Critias*', proving that this dialogue employs certain terms that do not appear elsewhere in Plato's works, terms that are borrowed from Herodotus.[19]

Such studies have confirmed the basic hypothesis that I put forward in the 1960s: namely, that the story of Athens's war against Atlantis, that is of the war of an Athens such as Plato would have wished it to be, is meant to represent a war waged between a so-called primitive or archaic Athens against the imperialist Athens that the city became after the Persian War, relying on its naval power. There are plenty of allusions to support that interpretation, such as the references to the Acropolis, to the temple of Poseidon and to the port that resembles the Piraeus so closely. Without restating all the details of this argument, suffice it to note that the country is divided into ten parts (*Critias* 116e) and that orichalcum 'was the most precious metal then known except gold' (*Critias* 114e). Atlantis is thereby credited with the ten tribes created by Cleisthenes and also with the Laurion silver mines.

More fundamentally though, the question is why Plato adopted a Herodotean guise. Why did he recount Athens's war against Atlantis as if speaking of the Persian Wars? The fact that he did so is indisputable. The gigantic scale of the army and fleet of Atlantis (*Critias* 118e–119b) evokes the similarly gigantic forces of Xerxes. The capital of Atlantis alone supplies, among other equipment, ten thousand chariots and two hundred vessels. However, the story of the Persian Wars is reversed. Here, Plataea, as it were, precedes Marathon. Athens starts off

> acting partly as leader of the Greeks and partly standing alone, by itself, when, deserted by all others, and after encountering the deadliest perils, it defeated the invaders and raised a trophy; whereby it saved from slavery such as were not yet enslaved, and all the rest of us [this is an Egyptian speaking] who dwell within the bounds [or pillars] of Heracles it ungrudgingly set free.
>
> (*Timaeus* 25b-c)

What Plato does not say and would indeed have been hard put to it to explain is how the Athenian hoplites vanquish the fleet of Atlantis. However, the—as it were—posthumous destinies of the two armies leave no room for doubt as to the fundamental opposition between land and water that permeates Plato's entire account. The war between Athens and Atlantis is followed by 'portentous earthquakes and floods, and one grievous day befell them when the whole body of your warriors was swallowed up by the earth and the island of Atlantis in like manner was swallowed up by the sea and vanished' (*Timaeus* 25c-d). Years ago, Joseph Bidez showed[20] that many of the 'exotic' features of the description of Atlantis are borrowed from Herodotus's pictures of the great cities of the East, Babylon, Susa and Ecbatana; on top of which, the very name Atlantis comes from Herodotus. Herodotus describes what lies to the west of what we call the Maghreb, after mentioning the Atarantes, 'the only men known to us who have no names' and who 'when the sun is exceeding high curse and most foully revile him, for that his burning heat afflicts their people and their land' (Book IV, 184).[21]

After a further ten days of travel, another salty hill, with some water near by, is reached. This hill too is inhabited. Alongside it lies a mountain named Atlas. It is narrow, perfectly rounded and so lofty that the summit is said to be always out of sight, enveloped in clouds in summer and winter alike. The inhabitants of this land say that it is the pillar that holds up the sky. These people are called the Atlantes. 'It is said that they eat no living creature and see no dreams in their sleep' (IV, 184). There are clearly several ways to read such a text, which is followed by a passage on the 'Pillars of Heracles', which are here situated on the African continent, not out to sea. But in my view, there is a clear connection between this perfectly rounded mountain and the precincts that Poseidon constructs as if using a potter's wheel.

Yet why has this connection so been seldom noted until recently? Probably because, particularly in France, there is too great a gap between historical and philosophical studies. The notion that a philosopher might take an interest in history and a historian in philosophy makes little headway in some quarters, although this does not necessarily indicate any disinclination to distinguish sources and arrange them in order of priority. Must we still, even today, bang on about 'the silence of Herodotus and Thucydides on the subject of Atlantis',[22] when for centuries it has been established that that continent was a pure fabrication on the part of Plato? Meanwhile, to argue, on the other hand, as if Plato had never read either Herodotus or Thucydides is altogether absurd. There can be no doubt that he had read them; but he then transformed them in his own fashion, which was not particularly favourable to positivist history such as that which—let us face it—Herodotus and Thucydides did, in their own ways, help to invent.[23]

Plato was perfectly at liberty to expunge Salamis from the history of the Persian Wars,[24] but for Herodotus and Thucydides that would have been unthinkable. Not that their history was devoid of ideological elements but, all the same, there were limits that could not be overstepped. In his *Archaeology* (I, 2–19), Thucydides introduced his historical theory of maritime imperialism but, of course, he could not speak of Atlantis because it had not yet been invented or even dreamed of.

Plato's oeuvre is and must remain our major source. Can pairs of oppositions parallel to those that construct the 'primitive' Athens/Atlantis pair be found elsewhere in the philosopher's writings? The answer must be an understandably qualified 'yes'.

At the end of Book VII of the *Republic*, Socrates, after expounding the theory of philosophers in power, reminds his listeners of the practical conditions in which such a city might be created. First it would be necessary to 'send out into the countryside' all those in the city over the age of 10, (VII, 540e–541a) leaving behind only those younger, who would, for the most part, have to be separated from their parents. Then, in Books VIII and IX, Plato sets out his theory regarding the four political regimes that are inferior to that of the ideal city: 1. a regime of the Spartan type, that is to say a timocracy; 2. an oligarchic regime, based on the possession of gold and silver; 3. a democratic regime; and 4. a constitution—if it can even be called that—that is tyrannical yet that would not preclude making a philosopher out of a tyrant, as Plato himself endeavoured to do with Dionysius I and Dionysius II of Syracuse.

Plato systematically explores how each regime emerges by modifying the previous one and also how the children of the previous regime turn into men of a different type. These are famous pages and worthy of admiration. Let me cite just one. It presents a democracy developing out of an oligarchy:

> When the rulers and the ruled are brought together on the march, in wayfaring, or in some other common undertaking, either a religious festival or a campaign, or as shipmates or fellow-soldiers or, for that matter, in actual battle, and observe one another, then the poor are

not in the least scorned by the rich but, on the contrary, do you not suppose it often happens that when a lean, sinewy, sunburnt pauper is stationed in battle beside a rich man bred in the shade and burdened with superfluous flesh, and sees him panting and helpless—do you not suppose that he will think that such fellows keep their wealth by the cowardice of the poor and that, when the latter are together in private, one will pass the word to another that those men are good for nothing?

Plato might almost have gone so far as to have had them say, 'We who are nothing, let us be everything!'[25]

But let there be no mistake: these pages are not pages of history. It would be ridiculous to reproach Plato for not knowing that in many cases an archaic tyranny preceded rather than followed the establishment of a democracy. He must have been as well aware of

4. Trireme, from the Lenormant bas-relief, Athens, Acropolis Museum.

that as we are, if only from the instance of Athens, where Cleisthenes created *isonomia* (equality before the law), which led to a democracy, *after* the fall of the Pisistratids, even if during this same period there were also instances of developments that took the reverse course. Plato was writing not history but political science, if I may use such an expression. How could Plato possibly envisage an ideal city turning into a city of the Spartan type, given that no ideal city ever existed apart from the primitive Athens of the *Timaeus* and the *Critias*, which had not yet been invented at the time when Plato was writing the *Republic*?

In truth, when writing of the introduction of *stasis*, faction or dissension, within *his* city, Plato himself produces a pastiche of Homer:

> How then, Glaucon, ... will disturbance arise in our city, and how will our helpers and rulers fall out and be at odds with one another and themselves? Shall we, like Homer, invoke the Muses to tell 'how faction first fell upon them' and say that these goddesses, playing with us and teasing us as if we were children, address us in lofty, mock-serious tragic style?
>
> (VIII 545d–e)

What better way of indicating that the famous nuptial number decoded with such scholarly care by A. Diès[26] is an elegant and scholarly kind of mathematical riddle?

The degenerate-and-perfect cities that form a pair are very close to the Atlantis-Athens pair but at the same time very distant: close because Plato certainly presents us with one legitimate city and others on the brink of catastrophe, yet very distant because, in the *Critias*, Plato is far more inventive than he is in the *Republic*. At the very least, it is fair to say that it is hard to define the political regime of Atlantis: it appears to be a kind of tenfold monarchy, controlled by a mysterious oath.

My second example comes from a text as famous as it is difficult: the myth in the *Statesman* (268d–274e). I studied it in 1975,[27] when I discussed it with Luc Brisson. In the end, it turned out that he had understood the text better than I had.

What is going on here? We are presented with two pairs of oppositions. On the one hand there is the age of Cronos, which is also a golden age, a cycle during which human beings, along with animals in general, are under the direct rule of Zeus's father. In this golden age, human beings are born old, from the earth, and proceed to grow younger and younger until they disappear. In this age of Cronos, men were, as Paul Valéry put it, 'white and sacred beasts', knowing nothing of cities or philosophy. In contrast, in the age of Zeus, our own age, human beings, aided by divine gifts (from Prometheus, Hephaestus and Athena), are capable of living in cities and philosophizing.

What I, along with most other interpreters, had not grasped was that the opposition between the age of Cronos and the age of Zeus should not be identified as an opposition between, on the one hand, a world left to its own devices and evolving toward 'the boundless sea of diversity' (273e) and, on the other, a world governed by the gods. Rather, Plato is here describing two *cycles* in which the cosmos turns now in one direction, now in the other, with cosmic catastrophes such as those described in the *Timaeus* developing at points when the direction is reversed. However, there are three eras: 1. the reign of Cronos (271c–272d); 2. the world left to itself and slipping toward pure diversity or Otherness (270c–271c), as Atlantis does; and 3. the world over which Zeus reimposes control (273e–274d).

Admittedly, in this text Plato is as perverse as he ever is. Resemblances and differences between the two myths leap to the eye. There are periodical catastrophes that accompany the cyclic changes and sweep away a large proportion of the human race. But in the Atlantis story, Athens, the city of the Same, and Atlantis, the empire in which Otherness develops, coincide in time, so both disappear in the course of the same catastrophe. Needless to say, Plato is well aware in the *Statesman*, as in the *Timaeus* and the *Critias*, that he is spinning a fable. There are three different levels to the myth; and just because the *Timaeus* is a 'likely' myth (29d) since the world of becoming cannot be an object of science, it does not follow that the *Timaeus* in its entirety is a hoax, as Jean Beaufret used to claim. On the contrary, I am convinced that there are elements of humour and even of the hoax likewise in the prologue to the *Timaeus*, the *Critias* and the myth in the *Statesman*.

However, it is to the *Laws* that we must turn for an explanation for a remarkable feature of the Atlantis myth. Why, in his description of the great island and its political institutions, did Plato include both eastern features, drawn from traditions relating to the Persian Empire, in particular in Herodotus, and also Athenian ones, thereby making the war between Athens and Atlantis at once a 'Persian' war and a civil war? In Books III and IV of the *Laws*, Plato tries, in his own way, to come to grips with real history. The various political regimes include two constitutions that are

> two mother-forms of constitution, so to call them, from which one may truly say all the rest are derived. Of these the one is properly termed monarchy, the other democracy, the extreme form (*akron*) of the former being the Persian polity, and of the latter, the Athenian; the rest are ... all, as I said, modifications of these two.
>
> (*Laws* 693e)[28]

Plato then goes on to explain that, in the past, Athens and Persia both achieved more or less 'the right balance', but subsequently departed from it. The Persians achieved that balance at the time of Cyrus, and Plato at this point seems almost inclined to echo the praises that Xenophon, in the *Cyropedia*, heaped upon the founding king. But however good a king Cyrus may have been, he 'entrusted his children to the womenfolk to rear up' (*Laws* 694d), with predictable consequences: his successors were 'over-pampered and undisciplined'

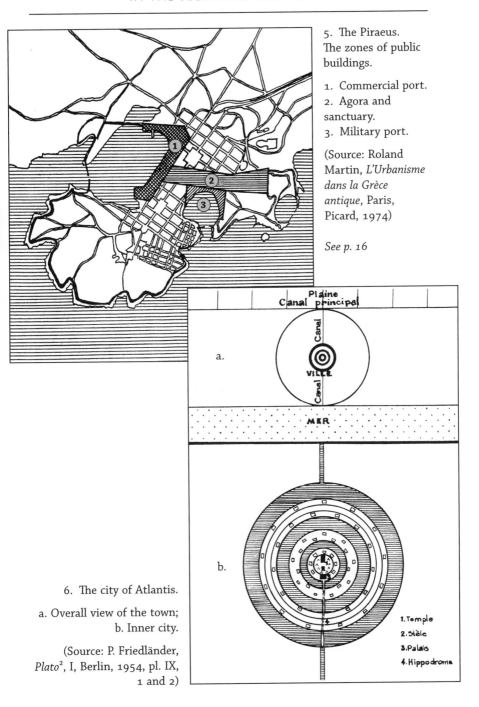

5. The Piraeus.
The zones of public buildings.

1. Commercial port.
2. Agora and sanctuary.
3. Military port.

(Source: Roland Martin, *L'Urbanisme dans la Grèce antique*, Paris, Picard, 1974)

See p. 16

a.

b.

6. The city of Atlantis.

a. Overall view of the town;
b. Inner city.

(Source: P. Friedländer, *Plato²*, I, Berlin, 1954, pl. IX, 1 and 2)

1.Temple
2.Stèle
3.Palais
4.Hippodrome

(*Laws* 695b). Darius restored the monarchy but Xerxes 'ended by repeating almost exactly the misfortunes of Cambyses' (*Laws* 695e). Athens, in contrast, illustrates the dangers of 'absolute liberty vis-à-vis all authority'. At the time of the Persian Wars, in the face of 'the vastness of the Persian armament that threatened us by both sea and land' (*Laws* 698b–c), danger strengthened unity and obedience to the magistrates. Salamis is cited as a chronological point of reference. The battle of Marathon had taken place ten years earlier (*Laws* 698c). When the Athenians learned of the preparations being made by Xerxes, they could think of only one way out: a repetition of the exploit at Marathon. There is no mention of Themistocles and the Athenian fleet. The Athenians embark not upon their ships, but upon 'their hope' (*Laws* 699b). And, as if he had not made the point clearly enough, in Book IV (707b–c). Plato declares that if Marathon and Plataea had won liberty for the Greeks, Artemision and Salamis made them cowardly.

All the above was by way of a follow-up to a polemic that had been raging ever since the fifth century and was not over yet.[29] Warfare at sea taught the hoplites to be cowardly (*Laws* 707a–e). In these circumstances, it is not hard to see why the primitive Athens is said to muster twenty thousand hoplites but has no fleet to stand up to Atlantis, which, for its part, possesses an enormous one.

Just a couple more remarks before we move on from Plato to his successors. As we moderns see it, Plato, with his story of Atlantis and its war against Athens, invented a genre that is still very much alive: science fiction. Of all the myths that he created, this is somehow the only one really to catch on. Nobody would dream of following in the footsteps of Er, the son of Armenius; and, even if Paris boasts its Champs-Elysées, we are well aware that those who dwell there are not the dead.

But there is also an art whose existence Plato anticipated, even though the technology for it was not yet available: the cinema. As is well known, the cave of Book VII of the *Republic* is constructed like a cinema hall,[30] in which the spectators are tied down. And in the *Timaeus*, Plato really does seem to be envisaging the cinematic principle. Here is what Socrates, after summarizing the conclusions of the *Republic*, goes on to say: 'Gladly would I listen to anyone who should depict in words our State contending against others in those struggles which States wage, and in how proper a spirit it enters upon war', with right on its side. But immediately before expressing this wish, he describes his frustration as follows:

> I may compare my feeling to something of this kind: suppose, for instance, that on seeing beautiful creatures, whether works of art or actually alive but in repose, a man should be moved with desire to behold them in motion and vigorously engaged in some such exercise as seemed suitable to their physique; well, that is the very feeling I have regarding the State that we have described.
>
> (*Timaeus* 19bc)

CHAPTER 2

THE ATLANTIS THEME
IN ANTIQUITY

Contrary to what might be expected, Atlantis was not a continent much frequented by Plato's successors.[1] Many seem simply to have scoffed at it. Theopompus of Chios, a young contemporary of Plato, was a by no means negligible historian. He was born in 378/377 and, as Dionysius of Halicarnassus (*Letter to Pompey*, 6) reports, 'he was an eye-witness of many events and conversed with many of the eminent men and generals of his day because of his profession as a historian, and also with popular leaders and philosophers.' Theopompus was the first historian to introduce philosophy into his writing of history. We know from both Athenaeus and from an inscription in Rhodes that he wrote a most ungenerous commentary on Plato, whom he accused of lying and plagiarism.[2] Meanwhile, so far as plagiarism went, he had himself transparently plagiarized the story told in the *Timaeus* and the *Critias*. In Theopompus's story, it is Midas of Phrygia, reputed by fable to have sprouted the ears of a donkey, who questions Silenus, who is represented as the leader of the satyrs and of Dionysus's entourage in satyr plays. Silenus tells of a great land, Meropia, inhabited by Meropes, that is to say mortals. Like the *Odyssey*'s land of the Cimmerians, Meropia had no day or night but, instead, a constant reddish dawn or dusk. Two symmetrical and antagonistic cities, with a vast expanse of land separating them, colonized this continent. The name of the one was Machimos, the warring land, that of the other Eusebia, the pious land. The former was imperialistic and had set about the conquest of the Hyperboreans; the latter was peace-loving and reaped the products of the earth without having to till it. Furthermore, the Meropes were blessed with two rivers, Pleasure and Sorrow (*Hedone* and *Lupe*). Whoever fed upon the products of the Lupe wasted away in tears, while whoever enjoyed the fruits of the trees that bordered the river of Pleasure lived his life in reverse order, starting old and ending up young. Theopompus was clearly familiar with not only Plato's *Critias* but also the myth told in the *Statesman*.

This ironical pastiche of the *Critias* was preserved by Aelian (*Historical Miscellany* III, 18).[3] Thanks to him, Theopompus's text passed down through the centuries, so that the ruins of Meropia and its towns even came to be known by the heroes of *Twenty Thousand Leagues under the Sea*. Without citing his sources, the same Aelian (*On the Characteristics of Animals* XV, 2) tells of the existence, beyond the straits of Bonifacio, of gigantic sea-rams whose horns served as crowns for the kings of Atlantis. The royal examples provided are reminiscent of the first kings of Macedon following the death of Alexander, which suggests that Aelian's source may be traced to the late Hellenistic period.

But, to return to Theopompus: what is striking about his text is that he replaces the Platonic allegory by another allegory, showing that he had understood the significance of Plato's one. Theopompus's story provoked the irony of the Christian Tertullian (*Adversus Hermogenem* 25.5).

Aristotle was a figure of a quite different calibre from Theopompus of Chios. Most scholars are content to follow Strabo, who contrasts Aristotle favourably with Poseidonias of Apamea (133–51 BC), a Stoic philosopher and geographer of the Hellenistic period. Strabo comments that the same applies to Plato and Atlantis as does to Homer and the wall constructed in the plain of Troy by the Achaeans: he cites Aristotle's comment (on Homer): whoever created it also destroyed it (Strabo II, 102 and XIII, 598). As regards Aristotle's position, we have one text in which it is clear that, even when presented with an opportunity to speak of Atlantis, he carefully avoided doing so. The text in question is of considerable importance since it is believed to have inspired Christopher Columbus to seek a direct route leading from Gibraltar to India and China. What exactly does Aristotle say?[4] He has just stated that the earth is both round and spherical and that it is not gigantic since different stars are seen as one journeys from south to north. He adds:

> For this reason those who imagine that the region around the Pillars of Heracles joins up to the regions of India and that in this way the ocean is one are not, it would seem, suggesting anything utterly incredible. They produce also in support of their contention the fact that elephants are a species found at the extremities of both lands, arguing that this phenomenon at the extremes is due to communication between the two.
>
> (*De Caelo* II, 14, 298a)

This is a powerful argument for, without naming Herodotus, it refutes him. Herodotus (III, 98–106) believed that the strangest and most marvellous regions were to be found at the outermost limits of the earth, for the very reason that they constituted its extremities. Aristotle reckoned that it was because the same sea joined Africa and Asia that elephants were to be found in both. At a stroke, given that the ends of the earth joined up, they were no longer its extremities.

In the *Critias* (114e–115a), elephants were said to be present in Atlantis thanks to the superabundant nature that provided more than enough to feed this animal which 'of its nature is the largest and the most voracious'. This mention of elephants suggests that, had Aristotle felt the slightest interest in Atlantis, this would have been a good opportunity for him to discuss it in detail and to offer his own description of what lay beyond the Pillars of Heracles. It was indeed a fine opportunity, but the point is that Aristotle did not seize it.

All the same, in his *Meteorologica* (II, 354a22),[5] Aristotle does explain that 'the water outside the Pillars of Heracles is shallow because of the mud but calm because the sea lies in a hollow'. On this point Aristotle, albeit with no interest in a submerged Atlantis, followed Plato, who described the straits as impassable, 'being blocked up by shoal mud which the island created as it settled down to the bottom of the sea' (*Timaeus* 25d). Obviously, on this point Aristotle allowed Plato to pull the wool over his eyes.

A collection of *Mirabilia* (Marvels) has also been ascribed to Aristotle. The source of many items in it is Theopompus.[6] One attentive sixteenth-century reader left a very meticulous summary of it, after expressing his doubts about its attribution to Aristotle:

> He [Pseudo-Aristotle] tells how some Carthaginians struck out across the Atlantic beyond the Straits of Gibraltar, sailed for a long time and finally discovered a large fertile island entirely clothed in woodlands and watered by great deep rivers but very far from any mainland; they and others after them, attracted by the richness and fertility of the soil, emigrated with their wives and children and started living there. The Carthaginian lords, seeing that their country was being gradually depopulated, expressly forbade any more to go there on pain of death and drove out those new settlers, fearing, it is said, that they would in time increase so greatly that they would supplant them and bring down their State.

This attentive reader-cum-translator was Michel de Montaigne,[7] writing in his chapter entitled 'On Cannibals' (Essays I, xxxi).

Hellenistic literature is one of scholars rather than researchers. There are exceptions to this, the most important of which—even including the philosophers—is Polybius. The same is true of Roman literature, again with a few major exceptions. Many works have been lost, one of the most important being the oeuvre of Poseidonius of Apamaea, a prolific polymath and the teacher of Strabo (whose oeuvre, for its part, has most fortunately been preserved). Poseidonius tends to be used as a handy stop-gap when one needs to posit a source for the transmission of letters. He has, however, on occasion been explicitly cited, as in the text mentioned above (Strabo II, 102), in which the geographer notes that Poseidonius had all the more reason to believe in the existence of Atlantis, given that Plato himself did. As we shall see, this whole discussion took place within the very Academy founded by Plato, where his deification had as yet reached only its early stages.

To the best of our knowledge, Diodorus Siculus[8] lived between 80 and 30 BC, which would make him ten years older than Virgil. He speaks of Atlantis as a follower of Herodotus rather than of Plato, and also of Euhemerus, a thinker who was a native of Messene in the early third century BC and the author of an imaginary journey in which the reader was told that the gods were former great men who had been carried to a higher level by the swell of collective admiration.

In Diodorus Siculus's *Library of History*, there is no Atlantis, in the Platonic sense of the word. Or rather, to be more precise, there occasionally seems to be some confusion between the Atlantidae, that is to say the daughters of Atlas, such as the *Odyssey*'s Calypso, and the Atlantes, a people of Libya who were neighbours to, and victims of, the Amazons. However, such confusion is dispelled once the manuscripts are corrected.[9] Diodorus does not name his source, who may have been an Alexandrian mythographer of the second century BC, a certain Dionysius of Mytilene known as 'Dionysius of the leather arms'. The general inspiration of these few pages (III, liv and lvi) is decidedly Euhemerist. The localization of the Atlantes is vague: all that Diodorus tells us on this score is that they 'inhabit the regions bordering the Ocean and possess a prosperous land'.[10]

In any case, the king who brings them out of a savage state and into an organized one is none other than an observer of the stars by the name of Ouranus. Ouranus founds a city, is able to predict the future, thanks to his skills as an astronomer, conquers most of the *oikoumene* (the known world) and from his several wives produces forty-five children, eighteen of whom are Titans. His daughter Basileia (Monarchy) has two splendid children, Helios and Selene, fathered by her brother Hyperion. The children are assassinated by their uncles, after which the Atlantes identify them as the Sun and the Moon. Their mother Basileia disappears in a storm and is then considered to be a goddess and receives sacrifices from the people. After the assassination of Hyperion, this magic African kingdom is divided up between his other sons, chief among them Atlas and Cronos (III, lx).

Atlas too is an expert in astrology and gives his name to the high mountain range mentioned by Herodotus. His son Hesperus disappears in the same way as Basileia and, in his turn, becomes a star, while his daughters, the Atlantidae 'founded the human race' (III, lx, 4). One of them gives birth to Hermes, a benefactor of the human race, fathered by a certain Zeus, while another Zeus, not the grandson of Cronos but his brother, engenders ten sons in Crete. These ten sons, fathered by Zeus (not Poseidon), constitute the only point of contact between Diodorus Siculus and Plato's story. But one can see how this might have given birth to the myth of the Cretan Atlantis briefly mentioned above.

However, the Zeus who is involved here is not the Olympian god. The latter, who took control of the whole world, was the son of a bandit called Cronos (a brother of Atlas) and his sister Rhea (III, lxi, 1). He succeeded his father, either when the latter stood down or following a popular revolt against Cronos the tyrant.

This is certainly a strange myth and it is only very tenuously linked with the Platonic one. However, Diodorus's text is the only one relating to Atlantis to come from sources other than Plato and Theopompus. Elsewhere, mentions of the Atlantis story invariably refer back to Plato.

That is certainly true in the case of a brief remark made by Pliny the Elder (*Natural History* II, 204–5), who observes that Nature is responsible for the fact that islands become detached from the mainland, as Cyprus was separated from Syria and Euboea from Boeotia; Pliny also notes cases of a reverse movement in which islands disappear and join up with terra firma, as at Epidaurus. There are likewise regions that become completely submerged, the principal example being Atlantis, which was swamped by the Atlantic ocean, 'if we are to believe Plato (si Platoni credimus)'. May one perhaps detect a hint of scepticism here?

Where Plutarch is concerned, there is no such hint. In his Life of Solon (26, 1; 31, 6–32, 2), he is in truth inclined even to outdo Plato. Unlike Plato, he situates Solon's voyage to Egypt in a period after his legislation; and he claims to know the names of the interlocutors with whom Solon discussed philosophy and from whom he heard the story of Atlantis. The priests were Psenopsis of Heliopolis and Sanchis of Saïs. Solon did try to introduce the story of the lost Atlantis 'in a poetical form to the Greeks' but, as Plutarch goes on to explain,

> Solon, after beginning his great work (logos) on the story or fable (muthos) of the lost Atlantis which, as he had heard from the learned men (logioi) of Saïs, particularly concerned the Athenians, abandoned it, not for lack of leisure ... but rather because of his old age, fearing the magnitude of the task ... Plato, ambitious to elaborate and adorn the subject of the lost Atlantis, as if it were the soil of a fair estate unoccupied but appropriately his by virtue of some kinship with Solon, began the work by laying out great porches, enclosures and courtyards, such as no story, tale, or poesy ever had before. But he was late in beginning, and ended his life before the work. Therefore the greater our delight in what he actually wrote, the greater our distress in view of what he left undone. For as the Olympieum in the city of Athens, so the tale of the lost Atlantis in the wisdom of Plato is the only one among many beautiful works to remain unfinished.[11]

This text clearly does not draw solely upon Plato. It incorporates at least one internal contradiction. The origin of the myth of Atlantis is first attributed to two learned men, one from Heliopolis, the other from Saïs; Plato only mentions learned men from Saïs. Furthermore, Plutarch makes the 'Atlantic' dialogue, that is the *Critias*, a work of Plato's extreme old age that was left unfinished. As I have already stated in Chapter 1, I myself do not believe it to be unfinished. If any dialogue of Plato's bears signs of incompletion, it is obviously the *Laws*, which are followed by the *Epinomis*, frequently attributed to Plato's 'secretary', Philip of Opus. But, whatever the case may be, the comparison of the *Critias* and the unfinished temple of Olympian Zeus is a superb literary flourish.

Later, around AD 200, Athenaeus of Naucratis, the author of a huge index in the form of a literary symposium, entitled *The Deipnosophists* (XIV, 690a) cites in relation to the word *metadorpia*, meaning a 'dessert', a short fragment from the *Critias* (115b) in which Plato uses the word: but this is a philologist's note, no more. Later still, the last of the great Roman historians, the stern and baroque Ammianus Marcellinus (XVII, 7) writes about the different kinds of earthquakes. Among them are eruptions so violent that an island 'vaster than Europe' was engulfed by the Atlantic Ocean.[12] The mention of Europe seems to indicate that Ammianus's comments do not stem directly from Plato. In contrast to Pliny the Elder, Ammianus Marcellinus manifests no scepticism at all as to the reality of 'the facts'.

However, at the time when Ammianus Marcellinus was writing, the second half of the fourth century AD, a huge change was taking place: the Roman Empire was turning into a Christian one, which meant that the spiritual ancestors of the emperor's subjects were no longer the heroes of the Trojan War but Abraham and Moses. In other words, Christians, who aspired to be the *verus Israel*, the one true Israel, now thought that history began not in Mycenae or Cnossus, but in Ur of the Chaldes and then continued in Jerusalem.

However, in order for the Graeco-Roman world to become Jewish, the Jews had first to become Greeks. As Elias Bickerman points out in an observation that I have often cited, 'the Jews became the people of the Book only when that book was translated into Greek'. It is a long story that begins in Alexandria but in which Jerusalem also plays a vital part.

The works of two Jewish authors of the first century have been transmitted to us not by the Jews, who for a long time sought to ignore them, but by Christians, who bequeathed to us texts written in Greek, in many cases in the Atticizing style. The two authors are Flavius Josephus and Philo of Alexandria. Josephus took no interest in Atlantis, but Philo did. Philo was an Alexandrian Jew who endeavoured to reconcile the authority of the Bible, in other words of Moses the Lawgiver, with that of the Greek philosophers from Plato down to the Stoics. As to chronology, Philo was plagued by no doubts at all. Moses established his laws 'long, long before Hesiod' (*makrois de chronois proteron*).[13] In the same treatise, known in Latin as the *De Aeternitate Mundi*, but whose title ought to be *On the Incorruptibility of the World*, Philo is led to refer briefly to the catastrophe in which Atlantis perished. He speaks of it in terms similar to those used by his near contemporary, Pliny the Elder.[14] What does Philo say? Having just reminded his readers that while some islands rise up out of the seas, others are swallowed up by it, he goes on to declare, 'The island of Atlantis, "greater than Libya and Asia put together", as Plato says in the *Timaeus*, "in a single day and night, through extraordinary earthquakes and floods, sank below the sea and suddenly disappeared", turning into a sea which was not navigable but full of abysses.' Philo's last remark suggests that he was not solely following Plato. Unlike both Plato and Aristotle, he makes no mention of the mud covering the vanished island-continent.[15] Had he done so, he would have raised problems of consistency with Biblical Antiquity and its tale of the great Flood.

However sure they were about the antiquity of their laws and their special relationship with the one true God who was their master, Jewish intellectuals nevertheless remained dependent upon those whom they attacked. For all that Flavius Josephus, in his

Against Apion (late first century) declares that Herodotus and the Greek historians as a whole are all liars, he does so in Greek. His response is that of a victim of colonization, comparable to the reaction of Algerian writers and historians who denounce French colonialism but do so in the language of their masters. Yet in the case of Flavius Josephus, there was, after all, a difference, for the Greeks were not his real masters, since they themselves were subjects of the Romans. In the second century, a certain Numenius of Apamaea was to snarl, 'What is Plato if not a Moses who speaks the Attic language?'[16]

The issue was taken up and re-elaborated by the apologists of Christianity (Tatian, Theophilus of Antioch and Clement of Alexandria). As representatives of the true Israel, they were in duty bound to take over the legacy of Israel according to the Ark that held their covenant with their Lord—at least right down to the time of the Incarnation. Down to the Incarnation but, of course, no further. Consider the case of an apologist such as Tertullian, who wrote an account of his literary and religious life between 196 and 222. He was a passionate and powerful orator who felt a certain sympathy with Pontius Pilate who, he claims, was already a Christian (*Apology* XXI, 24) and he described the Jews as persecutors (*Apology* XXI, 24). He nevertheless considered Moses to be 'about four hundred years before the time when Danaus, who is your [the Greeks'] most ancient of men, emigrated to Argos, and consequently before Saturn himself' (*Apology* XIX, 2). Tertullian was the first Christian to mention Atlantis. What did he say about it? Simply that, contrary to what empty-headed people believed, the Christians were in no way responsible for all catastrophes: 'If the Tiber reaches the walls, ... if the sky doesn't move or the earth does, if there is famine, if there is plague, the cry is at once "The Christians to the lions!"' Then, having pointed out that there was no lack of calamities in history, he adds, 'Plato tells of a land greater than Asia or Africa swept away by the Atlantic.'[17] Strikingly enough, while Tertullian reckoned that the Jews were the pivot of ancient history, he also thought that the Caesars, who reigned by the grace of god, were worthy of Christian prayers for their salvation (XXX, 1). Such was the first encounter between Christians and Atlantis.

Adopting the same line as Tertullian, the Christian orator Arnobius listed the catastrophes that had struck the world, ranging from scourges of locusts to the abduction of Helen, earthquakes and the fall of Atlantis, pointing out that they were nothing to do with the Christians. For Arnobius, the destruction of Atlantis was a historical event, just as were the conquests of Alexander.[18] He was writing at the very beginning of the fourth century, at the time of Diocletian's persecutions.[19]

One and a half centuries later, when the Roman West was beginning to crumble, Constantinople was the capital of a Roman Empire that could already be called Byzantine. This was the time of 'the last pagans' whose chronicles Pierre Chauvin has summarized with such verve.[20] Clearly, the paganism that Theodosius tried to eradicate in 392 was quite different from the paganism encountered by Cicero or even by Tertullian. The last anti-Christian Emperor, 'Julian the Apostate' (360–3) was a neo-Platonist rather than a follower of the traditional religion of the Greeks and the Romans. André Piganiol, in his *Empire Chrétien*, even calls him a saint.[21]

The weight of the State was immense, even—as my teacher Henri Marrou said—to the point of being totalitarian. But sometimes those in authority, whether pagan or Christian, while refusing to tolerate any 'political' life, in the Graeco-Roman sense of the word, would nevertheless express themselves at length in Platonic terms. The preamble to the 'Maximum Edict' appeared in 301, at the time of Diocletian, and fragments of this have been found scattered throughout the Empire, in particular at Ancyra (Ankara). They closely resemble the kind of *prooimion* (prelude) the theory and practice of which Plato discusses in his last, monumental, work, the *Laws*.

The fifth-century neo-Platonist, Proclus (412–85), wrote a commentary on the *Timaeus* that V. Rossi saw as displaying a 'speculative virtuosity comparable to that of Hegel', an epigraph that Father A.J. Festugière uses to preface his magnificent French translation of this commentary.[22] Half a century ago, Victor Goldschmidt who, along with Henri Marguerite, was one of my teachers in Platonic studies, used to tell me, 'Don't read Proclus. He's a pedant. Read Plotinus.' But once I discovered that Proclus had written a commentary not only on the *Timaeus* but also the *Critias*, there could be no question of my not reading him.

Before proceeding further, I should add that Proclus, like his teachers Iamblichus and, more directly, Syrianus, was as much a neo-Pythagorean as a neo-Platonist. In one of his earliest works, he refers to a so-called *Treatise on Nature* by 'Timaeus of Locri', which is, in truth, a first-century forgery, and he even repeats the accusation that Plato plagiarized it. A.E. Taylor who, in his own *Commentary on the Timaeus*,[23] insists that Plato was trying to express the ideas of a Pythagorean of the fifth century BC, is, in his own very particular way, a disciple of Proclus.

Eight centuries on from Plato, to what extent could Proclus get a handle on the author on whom he wrote a commentary? Where Plato is concerned, Proclus seems to suffer from one blind spot: namely, politics and everything concerning the *polis*, whether that *polis* be the one in which Plato himself lived or the one of which he paints a picture. In the prologue to his commentary, Proclus explains that the *Republic* represents the celestial order and he cites the famous statement that more or less brings Book IX to a close: '... the city whose establishment we have described, the city whose home is in the ideal, I think that it can be found nowhere on earth ... Perhaps there is a pattern of it laid up in heaven for him who wishes to contemplate it and, so beholding, to constitute himself its citizen' (*Republic* IX, 592b). Proclus adds that the war against Atlantis 'resembles the sublunary world produced by conflict and change'.[24]

Not only was Proclus a neo-Platonist; like Iamblichus, for example, he was also a neo-Pythagorean who speculated on numbers. The Pythagoreans maintained that the whole of physical creation was comprehended by numbers and all the works of Nature conformed to a numerical system (16, 20). Every number thus called for an explanation, whether it was the One, a dyad, a triad or the tetractus (the sum of the first four numbers). For instance, even the number of participants in a dialogue was of considerable significance. Proclus's remarks were based on what his teacher Syrianus used to say: when the number of listeners drops, 'discourse proceeds in a more secret and ineffable manner' (26, 7). In Proclus's view, it would be inept, here, to take literally Plato's remark that the fourth listener was absent on account of sickness.

Interest in numbers was not restricted to neo-Pythagorean circles. It is not surprising that speculation on numbers is called *geometria* by Iamblichus and *gamatrya* in the *Talmud*.

Proclus provides both a history of the interpretation of Atlantis and his own method of interpretation. Crantor, who was never a scholarch but did play an important role in the Academy of the second half of the fourth century BC, declared that

> Plato's contemporaries mocked him, saying that he did not invent his *Republic*, but had copied it from the institutions of the Egyptians and had thought what they said in mockery was so important that he had ascribed to the Egyptians this story about the Athenians and the Atlantes and had them say that the Athenians truly had lived under this regime at one point in the past.
>
> (76, 5–10)[25]

So, all this talk about the Atlantes was 'purely and simply a story', according to Crantor, who goes on to mention the inscribed stones that Solon saw in Egypt.

Proclus continues as follows: 'Others say that Atlantis is a fable, a fiction with no reality but one that does give some indication of realities that are eternal and that do come to be in the World' (76, 10). On this account they challenge Plato's famous assertions. At this point Proclus solemnly comments, 'Whatever is absolutely true is not partly true and partly not true, nor is it false according to appearances but true according to its inner meaning.' Curiously enough, Proclus does not cite any of those 'detractors' but at the end of his comments on Atlantis he does cite Aristotle (albeit without naming him) as reported by Strabo: 'We should not, therefore say that "once a proof is disproved, the subject in question is thereby obliterated", as Homer does in connection with the Phaeacians and the wall constructed by the Greeks, for those things were not imaginary fictions but absolutely true' (190, 5).[26]

However, Proclus's information about the 'real' Atlantis is extremely vague:

> That such and so great an island once existed is evident from what is said by certain travellers regarding what can be seen in the external sea [the Atlantic Ocean]. In their time there were, beneath that sea, seven islands dedicated to Persephone and also three others of immense extent, one of which was sacred to Pluto, another to Ammon, and one in between, dedicated to Poseidon, that was one thousand stades wide; and the inhabitants of this island preserved from their ancestors the memory of the Atlantic island that had existed there and truly was prodigiously great.
>
> (177, 10–20)

The only 'traveller' that Proclus names is a certain Marcellus whose existence is nowhere mentioned by any other author.[27] After speaking of those who deny the existence of Atlantis, Proclus mentions a number of authors, most of them Platonists, who detected in the conflict between Athens and Atlantis an analogy of a cosmic nature.

One of these is Amelius,[28] who explains rather too insistently that the primitive Athens is analogous to the fixed stars and Atlantis to the planets: for is not Atlantis divided into seven circles? Another is Origen, who detects in the Athens–Atlantis conflict a clash between two categories of demons, one side more numerous, the other more powerful and of better calibre. Similarly, Numenius of Apamaea, whom we have already encountered, sees the Athenians as noble souls, the people of Atlantis as souls attached to *genesis*. Porphyry believes that the West 'is a place of harmful demons'.

Proclus has much more to say about the beliefs of his teachers, Iamblichus and Syrianus: the opposition between the world of the One and that of the Dyad and between the Same and the Other, Movement and Rest, the Limited and the Limitless, is a cosmic one. This is the interpretation which Proclus himself finally adopts (and, as I have tried to show, it is indeed the interpretation to which Plato's text leads).

As usual, Proclus produces a wealth of analogies. He has correctly perceived the link with the Persian Wars:

> Since the Persian expedition came from the East against the Greeks, and particularly against the Athenians, Plato introduces the Atlantic war from the West, so that the city of the Athenians may be seen as a centre castigating disorderly barbaric multitudes pouring against it from both sides.
>
> (170, 10–20)

Over and above that human analogy he presents a divine one, with the Olympians on the Athenian side, the Titans (including Atlas) on the side of Atlantis. Furthermore, the Pillars of Hercules mark the frontier between the Same and the Other, and Proclus connects this with 'the boundless sea of diversity' to which the myth in the *Statesman* refers (273d). Proclus goes on to say: 'Matter is described by the worst of terms; it is said to be limitless, dark, irrational, immoderate, a principle of diversity and the dyad, just as the Atlantic ocean is named after Atlantis' (175, 20–5). Remarkably enough, whereas Diodorus and the 'Orphic' poets speak much of Crete, as do a number of modern scholars, Proclus makes just one dry comment on that island: 'Theologians usually regard Crete as a symbol of the unintelligible' (118, 25).

One emerges from Proclus's *Commentary* somewhat dazzled but also rather daunted by its incredible virtuosity, and disappointed by its dispatch of the political dimension, which Plato himself had, in fact, begun to destroy. Proclus does not refer to the Christians and if he happens to refer to Providence, he does so in the manner of the Stoics. If the Origen to whom he refers is the Christian one, he is the only Christian to be treated as a neo-Platonic philosopher (but that is a question that is still unresolved).

However, there is just one last Christian of Antiquity who is worth a mention. He calls himself a merchant and signs himself simply as 'a Christian'. He was a 'Nestorian', that is to say a heretic from the point of view of Christian orthodoxy as defined by the Council of Chalcedon (553). This Council decreed that the Monophysites fused the two natures of Christ excessively and that the Nestorians separated them too much. However, the above-mentioned Christian of course believed himself to be entirely orthodox. His *Christian Topography*, written in Alexandria between 547 and 549, carries the name of a certain Cosmas Indicopleustes in the eleventh-century manuscripts, but no such name appears in the more ancient manuscripts.[29] The name suggests that its bearer is a man of the cosmos, who has travelled in India. But in fact he does not seem to have ventured further than the Persian Gulf. His book is intended as a commentary on the cosmos that is directly in accord with the Bible. He believes that the world is oblong, in the shape of a puffed-up waffle and that the firmament is composed of a substance of a rigid nature (see Fig. 7, p. 51). So far as science goes, this work is extraordinarily regressive not only in relation to Proclus but also to ancient geography—Strabo, for example. However, the document is touching in that it testifies to a Christian popular culture; and its illustrations affected me rather in the same way as the sculptures

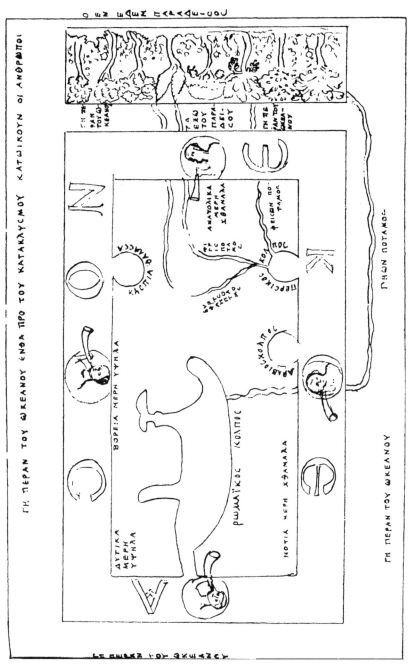

7. The world according to Cosmas Indicopleustes, Sixth century AD. (Source: *Cosmas Indicopleustes, Topographie chrétienne,* vol. I, ed. Wolska-Conus, Paris, Edition du Cerf, 1968)

of the Coptic Museum of ancient Cairo, some of which are contemporary with Cosmas and prefigure the development of Romanesque sculpture in the West.

The information that Cosmas provides on Atlantis is to be found in the last book of his work (Book 12, 2–8). It is presented as a commentary on the biblical Flood, which was known to the Chaldeans but not to the Greeks (apart from Timaeus):

> In similar fashion, Timaeus the philosopher mentions this distant land. He believes there was an island of indescribable size, Atlantis, situated beyond, in the ocean lying to the West, close to Gadeira (Cadiz). Ten kings who had come from the land beyond (*ek tēs peran gēs elthontes*) conquered Europe and Asia, having conscripted their inhabitants. Later, they were vanquished by the Athenians; and according to Timaeus, this island was then submerged in the waters by God's will. This Timaeus, of whom Plato and Aristotle approved and on whom Proclus wrote a commentary, expresses ideas similar to ours, but altering the *logos* [of Moses] and situating the West where the East is. He also mentions the ten generations and the land beyond the Ocean. In short, clearly all these writers borrow the story from Moses and present it as their own.

Having spoken respectfully of the Chaldean and Egyptian historians, who are 'more ancient than the Greeks',[30] our Christian writer continues as follows:

> The Greeks, in contrast, who came into the world after them, learnt to write only much later. Being settled far from the East, somewhere to the West, and living far from Judaea and Egypt, they knew nothing of these events, having neither seen nor heard of them. That is why they do not believe in the Divine Scriptures and consider the glories that they tell to be myths.

Fortunately, this situation was to change. The Greeks came to believe, but only later, thanks to the efforts of the apostles and the sight of their miracles. 'However, later on, as, with time, such signs ceased, you find many Greeks who used to believe and had been baptised believing no longer and paying no heed to the Old and the New Testaments.' Clearly they were men of little faith. 'So it was with justification that a certain Egyptian called Solomon told Plato, "The Greeks are eternal children; a Greek never grows up and among you people there is no really old teaching that has grown white with age".' (There is a twofold confusion here, first between Solon and Solomon and secondly between Solomon and the Egyptian priest.[31]) Whereas

> the whole of Ethiopia and the southern regions confirmed the Divine Scriptures, only the Greeks, with no wisdom apart from their own, knew nothing of their salvation. Only Timaeus, mentioned above, finding sources I know not where, possibly among the Chaldeans, recast their stories, telling of ten kings from that distant land, the island of Atlantis (which, according to him, became submerged) who conscripted the local peoples and, once arrived here, conquered Europe and Asia. All of which is a manifest invention (*hoper saphestaton esti plasma*). Since Timaeus was unable to show this land, he said it had been submerged by the will of God.

So it was all an invention, albeit one based on the Bible. As we shall see, similar arguments were to be put forward much later, in the Age of Enlightenment. Meanwhile we have at least learnt from the above what a Coptic Christian thought of the Greeks.

CHAPTER 3

THE RETURN OF THE ATLANTES, 1485–1710

C osmas was the last 'ancient' author to pass on to us the tradition of a myth of Atlantis, which he did in the strange manner described and cited above. Even if Plato did live on in Byzantium, there is no evidence that the story told in the *Timaeus* and the *Critias* was re-elaborated in any form there, except in glosses on Plato's texts. Besides, the *Greeks* of Byzantium were Romans. It is in connection with the West, rather, that, despite the various revivals of the Empire, one may speak of a broken history.[1] It is not the case that the *Timaeus* was unknown to Westerners. In the fourth century, it was partially translated into Latin by a certain Calcidius and it was both read and commented on;[2] and the stained-glass windows of western churches sometimes derived inspiration from the dialogue when they set out to depict how the world was made.

It has sometimes been suggested that traces of the myth can be found in the Irish legend of Saint Brendan.[3] Medieval maps specify a location for many mythical and semi-mythical countries ranging from Eden to the land of Gog and Magog and from the kingdom of Prester John to the place where the Antichrist is supposed, one day, to manifest himself. One example is provided by the Catalan Atlas of 1375, another by the 1459 map made by the Venetian Fra Mauro, produced in a century of great discoveries and commissioned by Alfonso of Portugal. But among those mythical places Atlantis does not figure.

An alert was first sounded in Florence in 1485, when the humanist Marsilio Ficino translated a number of Platonic dialogues, including the *Critias*. He decreed that the story was true—true at least in the Platonic sense which, however, certainly did not make it possible to show Atlantis on a map. Ficino's explanation of the story was based on the Bible.[4] A second alert was sounded when, in 1492, Christopher Columbus, possibly encouraged by Aristotle, believed that he had found a new route to India (although what he had really discovered was, of course, America). Was this a New World? As early as 1 November 1493, it was certainly declared to be so in a letter written by Piero Martirio d'Anghiera in Barcelona to Cardinal Ascanio.[5] The Atlantis bandwagon now began to roll, and there would be no stopping it.

As Claude Lévi-Strauss has splendidly described,

[A continent], hardly touched by mankind, lay open to men whose greed could no longer be satisfied in the other [continent]. A second Fall was about to bring everything into question: God, morality, and the law. Procedures at once simultaneous and contradictory were to confirm these things in fact, and refute them in law. The Garden of Eden was found to be true, for instance; likewise the ancients' Golden Age, the Fountain of Youth, Atlantis, the Gardens of the Hesperides, and the Fortunate Islands. But the spectacle ... made the European sceptical of [the existing notions of] revelation, salvation, morality and law.[6]

In *The Tempest*, Shakespeare was to call it a 'Brave New World'. See also Fig. 11 on page 70.

How was Atlantis fitted into this grand scenario?[7] By and large, the men of the sixteenth century approached the New World with two essential frameworks in mind. One had been formed by the Graeco-Roman tradition on which they had been nurtured, which included Plato's Atlantis; the other was the biblical tradition, which they regarded as the truth.

By 1527, Bartolomeo de las Casas, the famous bishop of Chiapas, who took up the cause of the Indians, was suggesting that it was reasonable to believe that at least part of the continent described by Plato had survived the disaster.[8]

Three years later, in 1530, a great Venetian naturalist, Gerolamo Fracastore, published in Verona a poem in Latin entitled *Syphilis, sive morbus Gallicus*, which means *The pox or French disease*.[9] Some Spaniards who had recently landed in America asked a 'native' priest the meaning of a sacrifice that he was carrying out for a crowd of sick people. 'The name of Atlas has probably come to your ears', he replied, recounting the story of his people, and went on to explain that the Atlantes had once been a happy people beloved of the gods. But when they grew wealthy they aroused the gods' anger, which was manifested by two punishments: on the one hand the sinking of Atlantis, on the other the spread of a terrible scourge, syphilis, among the survivors, that is to say the Americans. As G. Gliozzi has pointed out, this story is modelled on the prologue to the *Timaeus*. What is striking in the case of Fracastore is that there is nothing Christian about the reference to the gods. Instead, we find ourselves in the vast, free domain of mythology and fable.

If Plato provides one pole of reference here, the Bible provides at least three more. The central figure in the story according to the Bible is clearly Noah. All the branches of the human race sprang from his three sons, Shem, Ham and Japhet. In some versions of the story a fourth son, Jonathan, is added; but this extra son disappeared once the Bible printed by Gutenberg became widely available.[10] It proved extremely difficult to fit the Indians of America amongst Noah's descendants. However, this certainly had to be done once they had been recognized to be human beings, as was unavoidable whatever the obstacles, epistemological or otherwise.

The second myth of biblical origin was the extraordinary myth of the ten lost tribes of Israel. The origin of these traditions, which are still current today, is to be found in a biblical apocrypha (*Esdras* IV, 13, 40–4): 'The ten tribes crossed the river and found themselves in exile. They then decided to break away from the multitude of nations and to depart to some very distant place where no human being had ever lived.' As soon as America was discovered, it was regarded as one of the places in which the ten lost tribes might be lodged. Indeed, although Christopher Columbus had not been expecting to find America, he had taken the precaution of equipping himself with a Hebrew-speaking interpreter, in the person of his ship's doctor, Luis de Torres, a recently converted Jew.[11] So he was presumably expecting to encounter descendants of these lost Israelites in either India or China. This myth even overlapped with that of Atlantis, since the ten tribes were suspected of being responsible for the destruction of the island-continent.[12] Another theory was that Atlantis was none other than Palestine or the world before the Flood. This fitted in with Cosmas's *Christian Topography*; or so, at least, thought Jean de Serres (Serranus) whose edition of Plato was published by Estienne in Paris in 1578.[13] It was, for obvious reasons, above all in Spain that these questions were of the first importance, for Spaniards could now be regarded as a new chosen people, the more so since in 1492, the very year of Columbus's voyage, it had decided, through the Edict of Granada, to expel the Jews from the kingdom.

It was therefore in Spain, or in connection with Spain, the empire of Charles V and the kingdom of Philip II, that the debate on the New World, the Indians, their languages and their origins took off. In this domain as in many others, the ambassadors of Venice served as excellent witnesses. For instance, Gasparo Contarini, the ambassador to Charles V, speaking before the Senate on 16 November 1625 as an interested observer, described the splendour of the Aztec empire and deplored the cruelty of the Conquistadores.[14]

In 1552, Francisco Lopez de Gomara took on the role of an official spokesman. In his *Historia general de las Indias*, in which he cited the *Timaeus* and the *Critias* and, without really explaining the major contradiction with Plato in presenting Atlantis as surviving, attempted to show that the new lands could admirably be squared with Plato's story. To clinch the matter, he pointed out that the Mexican word for water was *atl*. Before this, in 1535, Gonzalo Fernandez de Oviedo, another spokesman of the royal court, had published a *Historia general y natural de las Indias*, in which he explained that the Antilles were none other than the Hesperides and belonged by full right to the Spanish crown. Charles V, who had been apprised of this in 1533, told the author of his satisfaction at learning 'that for three thousand and eighty years already, these lands have been royal property and that God, after so many years, has restored them to their owner'.[15]

A further step forward was taken by a Flemish subject of the king of Spain. In a posthumous text published in 1580, J. Van Gorp (Goropius Becanus) explained that ancient Tarsis, the Tarsis of both the Bible and Herodotus (Tartessos), the forerunner of modern Spain and the capital of Atlantis, had been founded by two brothers, Atlas-Tartessus and Odysseus-Hesperus, both of whom were grandsons of Japhet. The elder, Atlas, took precedence over his brother and his successors, the kings of Spain, thus clearly held rights over Atlantic Africa and America.[16]

Meanwhile, in 1572, Pedro Sarmiento de Gamboa produced a *Historia general llamada Indica* in which he similarly informed Philip II that, in the past, Atlantis, that is to say America, lay alongside Europe and, by divine right, belonged to him.[17]

In all fairness to human intelligence, it should be noted that it was also in Spain, in Seville, in 1589, that the *Natural and Moral History of the West Indies* by Father José de Acosta, one of the founders of ethnology, was published. Its author had the good sense to dissociate from America both the myth of Atlantis and the story of the ten tribes.[18]

As far as Atlantis was concerned, José de Acosta found at least one appreciative reader, in France, namely Michel de Montaigne. I cannot resist the pleasure of citing chapter XXXI of Book I of his *Essays*, the famous chapter 'On Cannibals':

We grasp at everything but clasp nothing but wind. Plato brings in
Solon to relate that he had learned from the priest of the town of Saïs
in Egypt how, long before the Flood, there was a vast island called
Atlantis right at the mouth of the Straits of Gibraltar, occupying an
area greater than Asia and Africa combined; the kings of that country,
who not only possessed that island but had spread on to the mainland
across the breadth of Africa as far as Egypt and the length of Europe
as far as Tuscany, planned to stride over into Asia and subdue all the
peoples bordering on the Mediterranean as far as the Black Sea. To
this end they had traversed Spain, Gaul and Italy and reached as far
as Greece when the Athenians withstood them; but soon after, those
Athenians, as well as the people of Atlantis and their island, were
engulfed in that Flood. It is most likely that that vast inundation
should have produced strange changes to the inhabitable areas of the
world; it is maintained that it was then that the sea cut off Sicily from
Italy ..., as well as Cyprus from Syria and the island of Negropontus
[Euboea] from the Boeotian mainland ... Yet there is little likelihood of
that island's being the new World which we have recently discovered,
for it was virtually touching Spain; it would be unbelievable for a flood
to force it back more than twelve hundred leagues to where it is now;
besides, our modern seamen have already all but discovered that it is
not an island but a mainland contiguous with ... lands lying beneath
both the Poles ....[19]

It is worth noting that Montaigne does not declare Atlantis to
be a Platonic fiction. He simply says that even if Atlantis had been
eroded, as had certain sites in the Dordogne region not far from
his home, that had nothing to do with America which, for its part,
was intact all the way from the Great North down to the Straits of
Magellan. Montaigne's reference to the Flood in this passage is the
sole indication that he had received a Christian education. He does
not mention any theories that link Atlantis to Palestine, but calls for
'pure' history and geography, adding: 'What we need is topographers
who would make detailed accounts of the places which they had
actually been to. But because they have the advantage over us of

having seen Palestine, they want to enjoy the right to tell us tales about all the rest of the world!'

Montaigne's rejection of a view of history and geography centred on Palestine could hardly be more clearly indicated and it shows that his thinking was considerably more advanced than that of many of the great minds of his own century and the next. G. Gliozzi, who in his book devotes to Montaigne a very interesting chapter entitled 'Montaigne: from Atlantis to the New World',[20] believes that the author of the *Essays* favoured a colonial venture very different from that of the Conquistadores. And it is true that in Book III, chapter VI, Montaigne writes:

> Oh, why did it not fall to Alexander and those ancient Greeks and Romans to make of it a most noble conquest; why did such a huge transfer of so many empires and such revolutions in the circumstances of so many peoples not fall into hands that would have gently polished those peoples, clearing away any wild weeds while encouraging and strengthening the good crops that Nature had brought forth among them, not only bringing to them their world's arts of farming the land and adorning their cities (in so far as they were lacking to them) but also bringing to the natives of those countries the virtues of the Romans and the Greeks?

The man who wrote those words was educated in Latin and also spoke French and Gascon. So he was well aware of his debt to Roman culture. But he respected the cannibals and reckoned that he himself had lived through times and wars far more barbaric than those described by the Westerners who had seen America. All the same, we cannot really expect him to be anti-colonialist before his time!

The famous humanist Justus Lipsius, who taught in the Netherlands first at the reformed University of Leiden and later at the Catholic University of Louvain, was also extremely critical of the Spanish conquerors, but he turned Atlantis into a kind of bridge that made it possible for Europe and Africa to communicate with America and also for the word of God to be spread in America, thereby restoring the authority of the Bible that Montaigne had undermined.[21]

Let us forge ahead. Francis Bacon (1561–1626) belonged to the generation after Montaigne (1533–92). When he died, he left an essay that was to be published in 1627 by his chaplain, W. Rawley. It was entitled *The New Atlantis*.[22] Like so many stories about Utopias, Bacon's book is an account of a journey not in the Atlantic, but in the southern seas. The narrator explains that his ship sailed from Peru and was bound for China, but a storm carried the crew, all good Christians, to the island of Bensalem. This island inherits a number of features from Plato's Atlantis, but has been converted by Saint Bartholomew. It is governed by scholarly men determined 'to roll back the limits of the human mind' (p. 72). The island is headed by a college of scholars, known as the House of Solomon. The population includes a number of Jews, 'very different' from those to be found in Europe, for they have the greatest respect for Jesus, even if they do not believe him to be the Messiah. These Jews are rather like Muslims.

The society of Bensalem is chaste and pure. Sexuality is satisfied in marriage alone and both polygamy and homosexuality are unknown. The inhabitants of Bensalem are not ascetics; they are sumptuously attired in clothing that evokes Venice. This is a society of scholars, something like the Museum of Alexandria or an ideal form of the French CNRS (Centre national de recherches scientifiques). Scientific investigations are pursued on the loftiest of mountain tops and also in the deepest of caves. Remarkably enough, mathematics does not constitute the dominant discipline. Neither Descartes, with all his quarrels with the person he knows as Verulam (that is, Bacon himself), nor Spinoza could have lived in Bensalem. Here, it is as if the imperialism of the Athenians and the Atlantes had been converted into a home for inventors, where Gutenberg, incidentally, has a statue. Microscopes are in use and the visitors are welcomed by Plato, no less, 'a famous man from where you live'.

8. Francis Bacon, an engraving by William Marshall, 1640. Paris, Bibliothèque nationale. Reproduced with the permission of BnF.

The inhabitants of Bensalem know Hebrew, Greek, classical Latin and Spanish. English is not mentioned, yet it is the language used to write this remarkable Utopia that is perhaps closer to Plato than may seem at first glance.

Bacon was a contemporary of Galileo (1564–1642). I have often heard Pierre Chaunu, a grand historian if ever there was one, explain, sometimes appropriately, sometimes not, that the framework for modernity was provided by two discoveries widely distant in time: one was the extension of space, a consequence of Galileo's innovative use of the *lunette* or telescope (1610); the other was Boucher de Perthes's discovery, in the early nineteenth century, of human fossils, a discovery that brought about the demise of the biblical chronology of the world, even if this continued to be taught in schools for many years. Without Galileo, Pascal could never have expressed his famous thought: 'The eternal silence of those infinite spaces terrifies me.'

Did perusal of the Platonic story in any way influence the seventeenth-century expansion of time? To my own surprise, I find I must reply 'Yes'. To extend time, it was necessary to destroy the biblical chronology, by showing either that Adam never existed or else that human beings had existed long before Adam.

This was a question that had been bitterly debated in late Antiquity, as Saint Augustine, for example, testifies.[23] The debate resumed in 1655 with the publication, in Amsterdam, a home to free thinking, of Isaac La Peyrère's *Préadamites*.[24] The work has often been the butt of mockery, thanks to the satirical epitaph that was aimed at him: *La Peyrère ici gît, ce bon Israélite/ Huguenot, Catholique, enfin Pré-Adamite,/ Quatre religions lui plurent à la fois, et son indifférence était si peu commune/ Qu'après quatre-vingt ans qu'il eut à faire un choix/ Le bonhomme partit et n'en choisit pas une.* (Here lies La Peyrère, that worthy Israelite,/ A Huguenot, a Catholic, even a Preadamite./Four religions took his fancy, all of them at once/And his indifference between them was so very strong/That after the eighty years he had in which to choose/The good chap passed away and never fixed on one.)

Although La Peyrère, who was born a Protestant, was obliged to convert in order to survive, and although he was an ardent partisan of the redemption of Israel, thereby continuing to attract readers even under Napoleon, he had, after all, been born a Protestant and he strove to prove that Adam was not the first man but simply the first Jew—a theory that elicited from Pascal an acerbic grouse on the subject of 'the extravagances of Apocalyptics, Preadamists, millenarians, and so on ...'. As I have indicated above, the theme of Atlantis prompted a certain degree of Spanish nationalism. La Peyrère, for his part, was a French nationalist who was of the opinion that the king of France was called to a messianic mission. We know Plato has Solon say that Atlantis existed 9,000 years before the Athenian lawgiver's visit to Egypt. This is precisely the fact upon which La Peyrère fastens in order to show that the human race existed long before Adam.[25] However, he establishes no link whatsoever between his own French nationalism and Atlantis. Plato said that Atlantis existed. There was no reason to discuss the matter further.

The national type of Atlantism that we have noted developing in Spain, where it survived in some form or other right down to the nineteenth century, also developed with extraordinary force in a country that had nothing in common with Spain apart from its Gothic roots: Sweden.

I now find myself obliged to speak of Olof Rudbeck (Fig. 16, p. 76). What does Thomas-Henri Martin have to say about this extraordinary figure, in the 'dissertation' that provided me with my point of departure in Chapter 1?:

Toward the end of the seventeenth century, a Swede of great learning, Olaüs Rudbeck, set out in quest of the great Platonic island. But instead of the Bible, he took the Edda as his guide. It did not lead to Judaea. All he needed to do was lift his eyes to his own country: he

9. Olof Rudbeck, the anatomist, and the revelation of Atlantis-Sweden.
Frontispiece of volume IV of the *Atlantica* (D.R.). *See p. 71*

discovered Atlantis in Sweden. He even claimed to have found, near Uppsala, the site of the capital of the Atlantes that is described in the *Critias*. The better to support this eminently patriotic theme, in his great mythological, historical and geographical work published in four in-folio volumes he endeavoured to prove that it was in Scandinavia that one should seek for the earliest origins of the peoples of Europe and Asia and the source of all their most ancient traditions. Rudbeck's theory became very influential despite the very limited availability of his oeuvre, particularly its last volumes. Quite a few solemn historians in Sweden were won over to his side.[26]

So let us now consider Rudbeck and his *magnum opus*: *Atlantica, sive Manheim, vero Japheti posteriorum sedes ac patria*, published in Uppsala between 1679 and 1702.[27] As the Latin title cited above indicates, the plan was to show that Atlantis, which Rudbeck equates with the human race (*Manheim*), was the seat and land of the descendants of Noah's son Japet (or Japhet) and (although the title is silent on this) that this seat was none other than Sweden. I have known Rudbeck's work for about forty years. It never ceases to fill me with the same alarm, but not because this is a paranoid thesis, for I am well used to such; nor can I see any advantage in describing its scholarly material as baroque. A certain kind of baroque art, such as the creation of Plato's cave, may be explained by the fact that the cinema had not yet been invented. However, the notion of a whole baroque strand of learning illuminates nothing. No, what disturbs me is that Rudbeck was a real scholar, a medical doctor and a professor who subsequently became Rector of the University of Uppsala, where he created a botanical garden and an anatomy theatre that still exist. He discovered lymphatic circulation; he was a Copernican; and he was among those instrumental in introducing Descartes's work in Sweden (see Fig. 16, p. 76).

Despite all this and although he remained a Christian, Rudbeck believed that Atlas, the son of Japhet, put down roots in Sweden and that all the other nations were fruits that had become detached from the stock of that genealogical tree. This man was an anatomist and a distant disciple of Vesalius, yet when he peered beneath the skin of Sweden he discovered Atlantis.[28] He reckoned that Scandinavian runes had preceded the letters of Phoenicia and Greece. He excluded Herodotus from the ranks of the world's explorers on the grounds that he made no mention of the Hyberboreans' civilizing role. The paradox, as Rudbeck saw it, was that it was through Plato that we knew this story about Atlantis, even though the Greeks had always lied to us. The long and the short of it is that, whatever the facts may be, Rudbeck simply replaced Israel, in its role of the chosen people, by Atlantis.

The greatest puzzle of all is that Rudbeck was taken seriously by plenty of clever people. In 1720, Newton asked to be sent a copy of his *Atlantica*.[29] Rudbeck was both a contemporary of Descartes and an initiate into a 'Gothic' type of nationalism that first made its appearance as early as the sixth century AD and that had made a great splash at the Council of Basel in 1434, when Bishop Nicolas Ragvaldi solemnly declared that the kingdom of Sweden was more ancient, stronger and nobler than any other. Far from being conquered by the monarchs of Rome, it had obliged the Romans themselves to enter into alliance with it. However, it was obviously in the seventeenth century, in the period of Swedish history known as that of the 'great power', when Gustavus Adolphus was king (1611–32), that Gothic primacy became *the* national myth of the Swedes.

Rudbeck himself dramatized the criticism that he was bound to attract, and he did so with considerable wit. He imagines a scene in which eminent doctors are discussing India in the presence of a little gardener (*hortolanus*). Presiding over the discussion is Apollo, no less.[30] Apollo and the great doctors have discoursed at length but the little gardener does not agree with them and dismisses all that he has heard as *chimerae atque deliramento*, fantasy and nonsense. 'That's as maybe', he says to his interlocutors, but we too, the likes of us, are men (*et nos homines*), even if the great doctors (*vos homines*) are

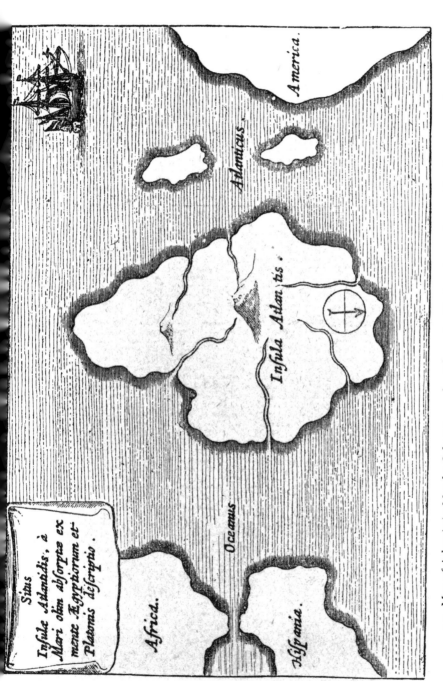

America.

Atlanticus.

Insula Atlantis.

Oceanus

Africa.

Hispania.

Situs
Insulæ Atlanticæ, à
Mari olim abforptæ ex
mente Ægyptiorum et
Platonis deſcriptio.

10. Map of Atlantis in *Mundus Subterraneus*, by Athanasius Kircher, Amsterdam, 1664. *See pp. 71 and 88*

ᴸ LE NOVVEAV MONDE.

'Eſt vne choſe plus qu'eſmerueillable, que ceſte partie appellée America, qui eſt quaſi la moitié de toute la terre, ait eſté incognuë aux Anciens, iuſques à l'an 1492. qu'elle a° eſté deſcouuerte par Chriſtoſlé Columbe. Car conſiderant la grande & laborieuſe diligence de noz predeceſſeurs, employée à la cognoiſſance & deſcription de la terre, comme nous voyons en Ptolemée, Strabon, Pline, Mela, & autres; ſemblablement l'opportune commodité qu'ont eu les grands Empires & Gouuernemens, comme celuy des Grecs & Romains, de chercher & trauerſer eſtranges pays & prouinces : enſemble la grande, deſmeſurée, & inſatiable conuoitiſe du genre humain, qui ne laiſſe rien à experimenter pour acquerir & conqueſter par art ou ſubtilité, ce dequoy ces pays cy de leur naturel abondent, à ſçauoir l'or : ſemble bien vne choſe plus qu'eſtrange, qu'iceux là, diſ-ie, nous ont eſté ſi longue eſpace de temps caché & incogneuz. Aucuns cuident que Plato ait voulu dire de ce pays, là où il eſcrit d'Atlantis. Autres penſent que Seneca ait propheciſé de ce trouuement en ſes Tragedies, par ces mots, *Venient annis. &c.* qui traduits en noſtre langue Françoiſe, veulent dire :

Apres pluſieurs années	La grand Mer produira
Vne autre aage viendra,	Terre neufue & ſeconde:
Qui par les deſtinées	Lors Tſland ne ſera
Pays nouueau monſtra	Plus la borne du Monde

Comme auſſi ces vers d'vne Sibylle, leſquels (comme eſcrit Iacobus Nauarchus) l'an 1505. ont eſté trouuez en Portugal ioignant la mer, aupres de Rochan de Sinna, engrauez en vne colomne quarrée, & commencent; *Voluentur ſaxa. &c.* ſignifiants en François ce qui s'enſuit :

> L'on verra en pierres lettres aſſez liſables
> Quand l'Occident verra d'Orient le threſor.
> Ganges, Indus, Tagus, auec autres encor
> S'entr'offriront leurs biens, choſes merueillables.

Marinæus Siculus eſcrit ſemblablement, qu'en ces terres neuues a eſté trouué vne medaille d'or, repreſentante la face d'Auguſte; & en ſigne de verité, il dit, que ladite medaille a eſté enuoyée par Sire Iolian Ruſus, Eueſque de Conſentia, au Pape; d'ont il ſembleroit, que du temps d'Auguſte iceux pays auroient eſté cogneus. Mais ie croy pluſtoſt que non, & qu'icelle medaille a parauenture eſté perduë d'aucun des Eſpaignolz, qui de noſtre temps y ſont venuz & arriuez, & depuis retrouuée. Touteſfois nous en laiſſons à chaſcun le ſien. Ces pays & terres neuues peu ſ'en faut qu'elles ne ſoyent totalement trauerſées & deſcouuertes, hors mis vers Septentrion, là où nous n'auoir eſté ſingléez, nous ſont encore incognuës. La figure de ce pays Amerique eſt ſemblable à deux Iſles, accouplées par le milieu d'vn petit deſtroict de terre ferme. La partie vers Septentrion comprend en ſoy la Nouuelle Eſpaigne, Floride, Terre neuue, & pluſieurs autres; l'autre partie vers Midy, contient Peru & Breſil. &c. Les Iſles appertenantes ſous ce pays d'Amerique, ſont; Spagnola, que l'on appelle pour le iourd'huy l'Iſle de S. Dominique; Cuba, & les autres circonuoiſines, qui ſont pluſieurs en nombre, & puis les Aſores, & les autres ſituées aupres de Terre neuue. Tout ce pays cy, qui a eſté deſcouuert & cognu, (excepté ce pays ſuſdit de Breſil, qui appartient au Roy de Portugal, & la Terre neuue, que tiennent les François) eſt de la Seigneurie du Roy d'Eſpaigne. Eſtâts ceſdits pays ſi abondants en or, qu'il ſemble incroyable, pource faut il que i'eſcriue icy trois choſes pour faire apparoir la verité. Premierement, ce que Gemme Phriſon eſcrit en ſa Carte vniuerſelle, à ſçauoir, que à Collao, ſitué au Peru, y a eu vne maiſon, de laquelle les parois & le toict eſtoient de pur or: Et ce qu'eſcrit Giraua, en vne prouince de Peru, appellée Anzema, les gens ſ'armer de toutes pieces d'harnois de fin or, comme nous faiſons pardeça de fer. Au meſme pays de Peru, les Eſpaignols (comme ils eſcriuent eux meſmes) ont fait ferrer leurs cheuaux de fer d'or, par faute de fer. De quoy ne ſe faut pas grandement eſbahir, ſ'il eſt vray ce que Giraua eſcrit, ſçauoir eſt, qu'aupres de Quito y a certaine Mine, qui contient plus d'or en ſoy, que de terre. Somme, ce ſont pays fort excellents & fertiles. Et entre autres choſes, ilz nous ont donné telle abondance de Sucre, que toutes cuiſines en ſont plaines, là où l'on le deuore par gloutonnie fort exceſſiuemét, au lieu que parauant il n'eſtoit recouurable qu'aux boutiques des Apoticaires, qui le gardoient pour les malades ſeulement, (par maniere de dire,) de ſorte que ce que iadis ſeroit de medicine, nous ſert pour le preſent de nourriture. Mais nous ne voulons pas omettre, que (deuant que la Nation Eſpaignole deſcouurit cedit pays) ils auoient grand beſoing de beſtes de ſeruice, qui aſſiſtent aux hommes; car il n'y auoit en leur pays ni Elephans, ni Chameaux, Cheuaux, Mulets, ni Aſnes, ou aucun autre beſtial portant fardeau, ou donnant du laict; excepté vn ſeul animal, que les Eſpaignols appellent vne Brebis de Peru, (tel que nous auons veu à Malines) de la grandeur d'vn Aſne, & de la façon bien pres d'vn Chameau, eſtant de couleur rouſſe.

11. A page from the French translation of the *Theatrum Orbis Terrarum* by Abraham Ortelius, 1595 (D.R.). In the very first lines, the New World is likened to Atlantis. *See p. 56*

no less so. On the frontispiece of his Atlas in volume IV, which is the last of his *Atlantica* (see Fig. 9, p. 66), Rudbeck arranged for the maxim '*et nos homines*' to be incorporated into the design, thereby casting himself in the role of the little gardener despite the fact that he was the very epitome of a great doctor who knew every available language and had read all the great books, yet perhaps who realized that he could be at the mercy of any little gardener. In the event, it was Pierre Bayle, exiled in Rotterdam,[31] who, in *Les Nouvelles de la république des letters* of January 1685, played the role of the little gardener, venturing simply to observe that a Frenchman, A. Audigier, had already insisted in similar fashion on the primacy of Gaul and hence of France.[32]

There had, in fact, been no lack of French ideologues who claimed France to be the kingdom of the chosen people: Guillaume Postel for one, in the sixteenth century, as well as Audigier who, for his part, considered Noah's real name to be Gallus.[33]

Gianbattista Vico was a citizen of a country (albeit one that was hardly more than a geographical expression), in which the Lombards were considered to be Goths and which could also fall back on the Etruscans, who were likewise serious candidates for the title of 'the princes of origins'. When writing his first book, *De Antiquissima Italorum Sapientia* (1710), Vico had briefly been tempted to adopt an argument similar to that of Rudbeck, whose works he had read, but had then thought better of it and instead proclaimed that all the nations (with the inevitable exception of the 'chosen people') are equal in the eyes of God and the cycle of history.[34]

Some of Rudbeck's contemporaries had questions to ask regarding Atlantis, but without imagining it to be their imaginary fatherland. The most extraordinary of these was probably a German Jesuit, Athanasius Kircher (1602–80). Like many others both before and after him, he regarded the Canaries as remnants of Atlantis. He produced a map (see Fig. 10, p. 69) of what he called the *Mundus Subterraneus*,[35] in which a prominent place was allotted to Atlantis.

12. According to Jacques Brunschwig's more than feasible interpretation, this is a representation of Atlantis. The only alternative—unlikely, given the iconographical context—would be Purgatory. Sixteenth-century fresco (artist unknown), "Labirinto d'acqua", Mantua, Ducal Palace (Sala dei Cavalli). Photograph supervised by the Mantua Patrimonio Storico, Artistico e Demeoetnoantropologico. Reproduced with permission of the Ministero per I Beni e le Attività Culturali.

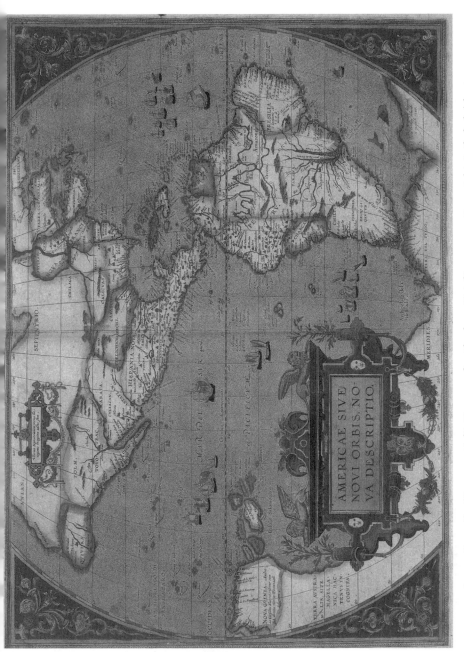

13. A map from the *Theatrum Orbis Terrarum* by Abraham Ortelius, 1595. Copyright Sotheby's/akg-images

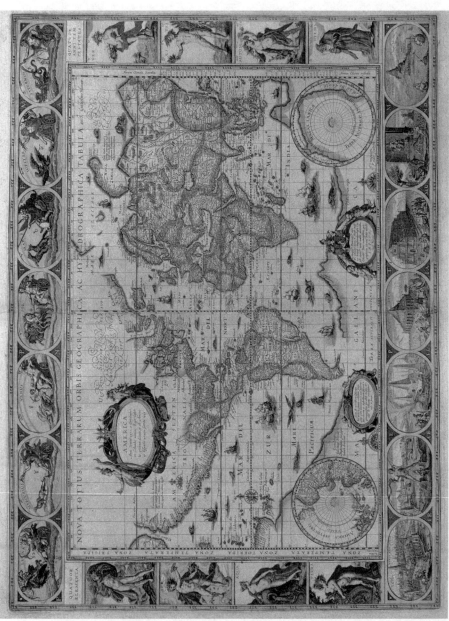

14. *Atlantis Appendex, by Willem Janszoon Blaeu, 1630. Copyright Søhlsby. (Above.)*

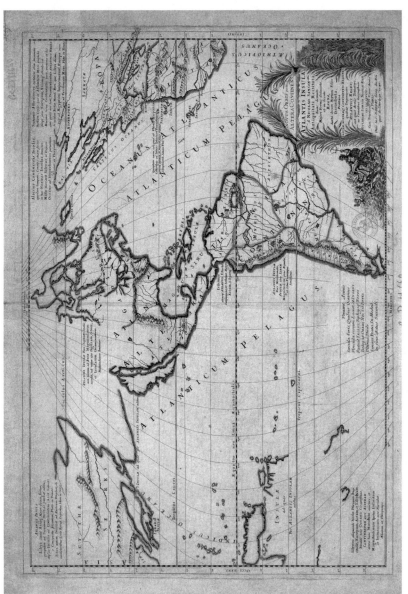

15. *Atlantis Insula*, map by Nicolas and Guillaume Sanson, 1668. Edited by Gilles Robert de Vaugondy in 1741. Photograph by the Bibliothèque nationale de France, Paris. Atlantis is situated, as by Bacon, to the west of America. Reproduced with the permission of BnF.

16. Olof Rudbeck, portrait attributed to Caspar Kenckel or Jan Klopper, 1687.
Stockholm, National Museum. *See p. 76ff.*

The Canaries were inhabited by a mysterious people, the Guanches, probably descendants of the survivors of the Atlantis epic. This was a hypothesis that was to be taken up again in the early nineteenth century.[36]

Let me repeat emphatically that Rudbeck, however bizarre in our eyes and in those of some of his contemporaries, Pierre Bayle for one, was by no means an isolated figure at a time when men such as Bacon before and Buffon after him were trying hard to situate human beings within nature. Before him, the Dane Niels Steensen (Nicolas Stenson), who was the first theorist of stratigraphy, had written as follows:

> I would not like to be won over too easily by the fabulous tales of the Ancients, but they do contain many things that I believe to be true. Consider, for example, a series of assertions whose falsity rather than truth seems to me questionable. For instance, the separation of the Mediterranean from the western ocean [the Atlantic], the existence of a link between the Mediterranean and the Red Sea, and the submersion of the island of Atlantis.[37]

In this connection, we shall presently see what a great source of inspiration the Flood, or rather Floods, were.

But first, since the Atlantes have returned, it is now time to see how they fared in the Age of the Enlightenment.

CHAPTER 4

THE ATLANTIS OF
THE ENLIGHTENMENT,
1680–1786

The question I now wish to address is lodged right at the heart of the movement of the *philosophes*. Was there, as has been claimed, a deliberate attempt to resuscitate paganism out of the remnants of Judaeo-Christian myths?[1] As we have seen, the strange work of Olof Rudbeck had gone some way in that direction; but Rudbeck had remained Christian. The death of Jesus on the cross was set alongside the onward march of the descendants of Atlas. As a key moment in universal history, it was not swept aside. To put the question another way: did the *philosophes* systematically destroy what the promoters of the 'Eusebian compromise' had set out to achieve, namely the integration of universal history into the dominant biblical tradition, an endeavour that Bossuet too was to undertake in spectacular fashion? If we accept that the answer to that question is 'Yes', we should bear in mind that ever since the fifteenth century educated men had had ancient mythology at their disposal and had put it to a variety of colourful uses. As Jean Starobinski has helpfully explained:

Given that the world of fable was pronounced by the spiritual authorities to be a profane world with no truly sacred content, no blasphemy or treason was involved when it was misrepresented ...

The duality of the sacred (which was Christian) and the profane (which was surrounded by a mythological setting) was such that one could play now on the separation between the two and their mutual exclusion, now on their parallelism and isomorphism.[2]

The question now raised, first by the Christians, then by their opponents, related to the unity of the religious history of mankind within a space which, since the recent great discoveries, had expanded beyond all expectations.

In 1680, Pierre-Daniel Huet, the bishop of Avranches, published his *Demonstratio Evangelica*, the book that, in a way, ignited the powder-keg. His purpose was simply to show that the biblical message had not been revealed solely through the lineage passing down from Abraham to Moses and from Moses on to Jesus, but that the ancient gods were also the heirs—albeit somewhat distorted ones—of Revelation.[3] As may be imagined, this was a method and a line of argument that could easily backfire. The *Demonstratio* vouchsafed a few words (p. 149) on Atlantis. They were based on the writings of Lopez de Gomara in the preceding century and concluded that the Mexicans were the heirs to the people of Atlantis. All the same, even if Huet, like others, did regard Plato as an Attic version of Moses, he did not take up the Palestinian interpretation of the myth.

Of course, with Huet, his successors and his opponents, we enter the domain neither of history nor criticism but gnosticism. Having selected a particular text, that of the *Critias* for example, as a starting point, the Gnostic would seek to uncover some deeply buried secret. Many years previously, the Apocalypse of Saint John had been one such text. Rudbeck's work, which I have analysed in Chapter 3, was an attempt to eliminate Herodotus from historiography, to turn Plato into a source for the history of Scandinavia, and to shift Atlantis from the extreme West to the Far North. The completion of such an agenda was by no means child's play!

Those who succeded Huet and had to face up to the *philosophes* and the new pagans resurrected the old idea according to which Atlantis constituted a covert description of Palestine. This was the line adopted by Claude Olivier, a Marseilles lawyer who in 1726 explained, with some success, that it was 'more likely that Solon spoke with the Egyptian priests of the history of the Hebrews than that of Mexico'. He then proceeded to develop the following extraordinary argument: the island of Atlantis was divided into ten parts since there were ten tribes of Israel on this side of the river Jordan. Ruben and Gad, which were situated in what is now Transjordania, 'would have been less known among the Egyptians'.[4]

Olivier's hypothesis stemmed, without the author realizing it, from Cosmas Indicopleustes, but at some remove. It was seized upon in northern Europe, where it clashed with the great national myth created by Rudbeck. It was left to H. Scharban to open the ball (or rather to open fire), in Lübeck in 1733,[5] and he was closely followed by two Swedish pastors, one of whom, F. Bauer, wrote in French, thereby relaunching the debate among the *philosophes*.[6]

Following the line taken by F. Bauer but within Catholic circles that would today be described as fundamentalist, a series of researchers attacked Herodotus and also 'the eighteenth-century Herodotus', who was none other than Voltaire. One of these attackers was Abbé Jacques-Julien Bonnaud whose master-work, *Hérodote historien du people hébreu sans le savoir* (Herodotus, unknowingly the historian of the Hebrew people), was published in the Hague in 1786. He recognized that the Protestant F. Bauer was right, for he had 'shown that this piece by Plato was simply an adaptation from Moses and that this Atlantis had never existed and could basically be reduced to a disguised description of Judaea': not that this should prevent one from reading 'the divine Plato' with pleasure. Bonnaud provides a particularly provocative example of the type of attacks that a whole group of priests (Guérin du Rocher, L. Chapelle and Para du Phanjas)[7] were at this point launching against the *philosophes*. Even today, such speculations still circulate in various fundamentalist circles, both Protestant and Jewish, particularly in the United States and Israel.

All this made Voltaire laugh: 'Above all, it seems most likely that Sesostris is none other than the Hebrew Joseph. But having proved that Sesostris may have been Joseph, Monsieur Guérin then proves that Sesostris may have been Jacob, so in all probability the Jews have taught the whole world'.[8]

The above theory, which was based on the second- and third-century theologians of Alexandria, was meaningful only to Christians. But among the intellectual descendants of Rudbeck, there were other nationalistic Gnostics. Let me cite the work of one of these, Count Gian Rinaldi Carli (1720–95), who was singing the praises of Italy long before its political unification and who, many years before Gioberti and his *Primato* (1843) on Italy, was already presenting his native land both as the heir to Atlantis and as the fount of ancient wisdom.

Eighteenth-century Italy was a field strewn with ruins overrun by speculators in quest of a distant golden age. Over and above the evidence provided by the papacy that had been grafted on to the Roman Empire, there were the Etruscans, the Greeks, the Italic people, and the Celts of ancient Cisalpine Gaul, now Lombardy, any one of which could well have sown the seeds of civilization and produced a non-biblical Eden.

The fact that such research was pursued in Italy and elsewhere too is by no means surprising. Nor, after what had happened in Spain and Sweden, was it surprising that this return to a distant past should take the form of an Italian adaptation of the myth of Atlantis: in default of a myth of autochthony or one to compete with it, recourse to an imported myth was altogether to be expected. But what complicated things and made them less predictable was the merging of national myths and reflection on America. The second half of the eighteenth century in Europe saw the debate on America take off once more: was America the land of a virgin human race that had escaped the curse of the civilized societies that were marked more or less consciously by original sin, or was it, on the contrary, a region that was only marginally human? Was it evidence of a golden age or of a damnation? Atlantis, which for some people had been American ever since the sixteenth century, quite naturally slipped into the dispute.[9]

What is more surprising and unexpected is to find Carli intermingling the two themes in a more or less adroit fashion. His Atlantis is at once Italian and American, both at the same time.[10] There was even a Hebrew dimension to his Atlantis: the word 'Amazon' that designates a Peruvian people is a Hebrew word.[11] How did the valiant count come up with such a remarkable result? To borrow, once again, an expression commonly used by the likes of soldiers and policemen, this was certainly not 'child's play' or 'a job for amateurs'. He had to assume that long ago the continent whose destruction Plato had related used to link the Mediterranean and America. In this way, Italy was in communication with both Greece and America. This was how it was *before the Etruscans* and, of course, before the Celts. The successor to the aboriginal King Janus was Saturn, and he came to Italy at the head of the peoples of Atlantis.[12] Not even Euhemerus or Diodorus could have invented all this. Carli thus concluded that it was from America that civilization had come to the Mediterranean world.

Carli was as forthright as could be desired as to his nation-alistic motivations. 'Here in Italy, we seek to owe everything to foreign peoples, above all to the barbarians whom we claim as our ancestors':[13] a very strange line of reasoning, it must be said, as if having civilizing heroes come from distant Atlantis was a way of opting for autochthony. In his own way, Carli rejected the Jewish tradition: according to him, the flood that swept away Atlantis *was not* the flood of Genesis. He likewise rejected the Greek tradition, in particular Herodotus who, according to him, clearly did not know Europe.[14] Of course, Carli also criticizes Rudbeck's Nordic interpretation, including its more universalist versions such as one produced by Bailly, to which I shall return. How could Enlightenment possibly have come from the North? Nor did it come from the East. The true cradle of civilized humanity was America-Atlantis: even the Hebrews had benefited from it and inherited it.[15] Carli believed that, in this way, he had proved his point, namely that enlightenment reached mankind by way of the Italians.[16]

Carli was not Rudbeck's only Atlanto-nationalist successor. We shall be considering others in Chapter 5, which is devoted to the nineteenth century, the age of nations *par excellence*. But some countries were provisionally spared such writers. One such was England, where Bacon's *New Atlantis* had seen the light of day. J. Harrington's *Oceana* (1656) was dedicated to Cromwell, who was later to cast its author into prison. When it was eventually possible to publish the work, at the beginning of the eighteenth century, John Toland noted that it was written 'as an imitation of Plato's story of Atlantis'. However, in truth, this apologia for a republican and trading England had nothing at all in common with Plato's story, apart from the fact that it could be classified as belonging to the same literary genre.

However, the Age of Enlightenment did produce a few versions of Atlantis that were neither biblical nor nationalist. One was a work entitled *Le Monde primitif* (The Primitive World),[17] which explained that civilization may well have arisen simultaneously in China, India and the Near East. Was the matrix of the human race (*vagina gentium*), of which Jordanes spoke in connection with Scandinavia at the time of the collapse of the Roman Empire, really situated in the ancient world and, if so, could it not have spread in the direction of all these three regions of the Near and Far East? When Voltaire speaks, in *Le Mondain*, of 'the blessed times of Saturn and Rhea', he gives thanks to 'wise Nature which has had him born, to his advantage, in this age so decried by our wretched censors'. But is that really the age of Voltaire or a far more ancient one?

Now let us follow the line adopted by Jean-Sylvain Bailly, an astronomer and historian of astronomy who in 1789 became the first mayor of Paris before perishing, like so many others, beneath the guillotine. He set out on the track of civilization as it appeared in China, in India, and in the Mesopotamian Near East, returning to his theme in a whole series of works [18] and arguing that those different forms of civilization must have shared a common origin. In opposition to Voltaire who, playfully rather than seriously, favoured the primacy of India ('I am convinced that everything comes from the banks of the Ganges'),[19] Bailly persisted in his quest for 'a destroyed and forgotten group who had preceded and enlightened even the most ancient of peoples'. To please Voltaire, he was prepared to accept that the philosophy of the Greeks was that of the 'Brahmins', 'But was that enlightenment really born in India? Was it not just as likely to have originated in China or in Chaldaea?'[20] For even if we accept that the first language was Sanskrit, that is a dead language [not true, actually] and a dead language implies a destroyed people.[21] Bailly located his people further to the North and the East than Rudbeck's Sweden. His reasons for doing so were geographical. He argued that, coming from the Far North, the waves of civilization were more likely to spread out in all directions. However, he formally rejected a diffusionist hypothesis: 'The conformities were not produced by direct communication.'[22] He identified this primitive people neither as the Swedes nor as the Jews,[23] but as Atlantes. According to Bailly, what Plato describes is quite simply the memory of a golden age: 'This beguiling fable is thus just a preserved memory of a land long abandoned but still beloved.'[24] Alternatively, that golden age might lie in the future: 'If ever we find the country of the Atlantes, we shall know the land where our ancestors were so happy.'

By our ancestors, Bailly meant the ancestors of most human beings, since, for neither love nor money, was he a nationalist: 'Our worthy Gauls are descended, like other peoples, from a country common to us all.'[25] Naturally, assertions such as Bailly's presupposed a somewhat strange manipulation of the texts. One had to accept, for example, that Herodotus identifies the Red Sea with the Atlantic Ocean—a hypothesis that is about as ridiculous as Rudbeck's fantastical tales.[26]

As for Plato, from whom this whole tradition came down to us, he remains an elusive figure. For one thing, we are supposed to believe him to have been an inhabitant of India,[27] for another, his account needs to be decoded 'because he could not have expressed himself better had he wished to mislead posterity'.[28] In Bailly's view, situating Atlantis to the west was a deliberately misleading ploy. His Atlantis thus plays a double role: it is both a substitute for Judaea and a real counterpart of the biblical Eden. However, contemporary criticism was not fooled. After refuting Bailly with a number of solid scholarly arguments, one Catholic commentator wrote as follows in the *Journal des savants*: 'In this way, the Hebrew people is totally denied the prerogative of having enlightened the nations, as almost all respectable scholars had hitherto believed.'[29]

And what of the historians? There is no denying that this discipline that we hold so dear was throughout the eighteenth century by no means homogeneous. But then, is it any more so, even today? Momigliano[30] suggests that a fundamental turning point was reached in 1776, when Gibbon began to write his *History of the Decline and Fall of the Roman Empire*, for this work managed to combine the art of narration with the most scholarly erudition, as practised by Lenain de Tillemont at the very beginning of the eighteenth century. But it was really the following century that was to be the great age for history.

We have noted that the historical genre was by no means all of a piece in the Age of Enlightenment; nevertheless, we should not exclude from the present study either a writer such as Voltaire or an erudite scholar who, though famous in his own day, is less so now: namely, Nicolas Fréret (1688–1749) who, at his death, held the post of permanent secretary of the Académie des Inscriptions et Belles-Lettres.[31] Both these authors deserve to have a few words devoted to them.

Nicolas Fréret was a secular intellectual in the tradition of the great erudite Dutch scholars of the seventeenth century. He was read and valued by the men of the Enlightenment but, although he was imprisoned in the Bastille for a while, he was never, strictly speaking, a *philosophe*. When he spoke up on the subject of Atlantis,[32] in connection with the idea of a series of Floods, he expressed a radical scepticism:

> Plato had to say what he did about these floods and their consequences in order to lend some credibility, in his fable of Atlantis, to the greatness and power of the ancient town of Athens and to the fertility of the land of Attica. Given that none of the events had taken place in his own time and that there remained not even any vestiges of the Atlantic island, he had to find some reply to objections on that score … The damage caused by the three successive floods that changed the face of Europe provided him with a solution. If the modern authors who have tried to find Plato's island of Atlantis in America had spared some thought for the general design of the *Timaeus* and the *Critias*, they would have realized that the whole thing should be regarded as a philosophical fiction.

One cannot say fairer than that! Many misguided writers of his own time, of subsequent ages and also of today would have been very well advised to read Fréret before putting pen to paper.

Voltaire adopts a lighter tone. At the very beginning of his *Essai sur les moeurs* (1769), he simply writes,

> The greatest of all these upheavals would be the loss of the land of Atlantis if it were true that such a part of the world ever existed. Most likely it was none other than the island of Madeira, which may have been discovered by the Phoenicians, the boldest seamen of Antiquity, but was then forgotten, eventually to be rediscovered in the fifteenth century AD.[33]

On the subject of Atlantis, geography, then taking its first steps, adopted a similar line to that of Voltaire or, better still, Fréret. D'Anville, for example, wrote as follows: 'Why not ascribe Plato's narrative to an Athenian who wished to celebrate his own land, and what he says about the organization of Atlantis to a philosopher indulging in speculation more magnificent than realistic?'[34]

Ever since the Portuguese and Spanish explorations during the Renaissance, Madeira, the Canaries and the Azores had figured as likely hypotheses for the interpretation of the Timaeus and the Critias. So Voltaire cannot be said to be particularly innovative in this respect. In the seventeenth century, the German Jesuit Athanasius Kircher (1602–80), who was the first to produce a map of Atlantis (see Fig. 10, p. 69), had, in his Subterranean World,[35] set out the hypothesis that the Guanches, the Spaniards' predecessors in the Canary Isles, might be survivors from the epic of Atlantis. In the nineteenth century, that hypothesis still found a scholarly supporter,[36] and it is one that even today is encountered among more or less well-informed specialists.[37] It becomes more complicated, in a more or less secularized form, among certain theorists of the catastrophe. For example, J. Pitton de Tourneford, the famous traveller in the East, explains that the opening up of the straits of Gibraltar was a consequence of a more ancient rupture that had created the Bosphorus:

> Perhaps the horrifying eruption that occurred in the ocean at that time submerged or swept away the famous island of Atlantis that Plato described ... The Canary Isles, the Azores and America may constitute what remains of it; so it would not be surprising to find that they are populated by descendants of Adam or Noah, nor that their peoples use the same weaponry as other peoples of Asia and Europe.[38]

At the dawn of the eighteenth century, as in the two preceding centuries, the quest for Atlantis could thus still be combined with the biblical legend about the sons of Noah.

Let me now introduce two figures from the Age of Enlightenment who stand out by reason of their extreme originality. By the end of the century one of them, Nicolas Boulanger (1722–59) enjoyed an illustrious reputation that was altogether spurious since members of the 'Holbachian coterie', as Jean-Jacques Rousseau called them, had published under his name a number of works of which Boulanger himself had written not so much as a line. The other, the Piedmontese Giuseppe Bartoli (born in Padua 1717, died in Paris 1788) was, to put it mildly, hardly known at all either in his own century or in those that followed.

Nicolas Boulanger, who received his diploma from the Grande Ecole des Ponts et Chaussées only on the point of retirement, in 1758, shortly before his death (on 16 September 1759), was in every respect a most unusual figure.[39] Intellectually, he was immensely ambitious. He wished to lay down the law, not on the present, but on what he called Antiquity, in as much as it was a period that had experienced such remarkable cosmic upheavals as the floods, about which he had read not only in the Bible but also in Plato's works, the *Timaeus*, the *Laws*, the *Critias* and the *Statesman*. Although Plato is not the author that Boulanger cites the most frequently, he is unquestionably the one who provided him with the historico-cosmological framework that he needed.

When I was applying myself to a little geography, as a necessary accompaniment to my graduate studies in history, I was taught by Jean Dresch, whose advice to his students, whatever their subject, whether it was the population of Brazil or some little river peacefully flowing through stands of poplars, was 'Look for the drama! (*Cherchez le drame*)'. What he meant by drama was what others called dialectic. Boulanger, for his part, went in search of the drama of water, since— as he saw it—the entire history of Antiquity, that is to say not just Greece and Rome, but the history or prehistory of the whole planet, revolved around a succession of floods. According to Boulanger, the 'great secret' of the history of the human race was that after each periodical catastrophe, a 'despot' who was also a religious lawgiver appeared, to govern his fellow human beings. Moses was one of these, but there was nothing exceptional about him. As for the purpose of religion, it was to mask the fear of a return of disasters, despite the fact that such a return was inevitable, as is proved by the existence of marine fossils in inland places far from any sea. These testify to a prehistory that Boulanger discovered long before Boucher de Perthes, a writer of the early nineteenth century, but long after Xenophanes of Colophon (Diels-Kranz, *Vorsokratiker* 21 A 33).

> Faced with the great spectacle of a universe destroyed and then restored before their eyes, men set up a Religion, the principal motive of which was to express infinite gratitude toward the supreme Being who had saved them ... To perpetuate the memory of the upheavals that had occurred, they instituted commemorative festivals which, through the details that they represented, were of a kind to remind the Nations constantly of the fragility of their existence on this earth and warn them, by representing the vicissitudes of the past, of all those to come.[40]

In the same text, Boulanger explains, 'The commemoration of nature's revolutions, either through water or through fire, was the original intention and earliest object of all the festivals of Antiquity, whatever form they took and among whatever peoples we find them.'[41] We should note that fire is mentioned only in the interest of symmetry, a false symmetry that likens Boulanger to Plato. But there is no mention at all of a vengeful God or a flood sent as a punishment, such as the one recorded in the Bible, from which Noah was saved. Instead, Boulanger writes of floods that occur periodically, like the one of which Plato tells: the secret of the universe is that, periodically, Nature becomes the enemy of the human race. Floods recur eternally and it makes no difference whether it is the Deucalion of the Greeks who is involved or the Noah of the Jews.[42] The coming of the Great Judge, the judge of the Apocalypse for example, and the expectation of the Messiah constitute culturally shaped expressions of the fear of the recurrence of the Flood.

And what is the place of Atlantis in all this? To judge from the studies that I have cited, Boulanger never mentions it. However, P. Sandrin has now unearthed a manuscript by Boulanger preserved in the Musée de Paris,[43] a manuscript copiously plagiarized (although never mentioned) by Buffon in his *Epoques de la nature*.[44] But even before this discovery, Buffon had declared in his thesis, 'Earlier civilizations had been swallowed up by the waters but Boulanger, being a reasonable man, did not allow himself to dream of that Atlantis of so long ago'.[45] We now know that Boulanger, however reasonable a man and whether or not a dreamer, did in fact speak of Atlantis.[46] And what did the story that Plato related in the *Timaeus* and the *Critias* tell the author of *Les Anecdotes de la nature*? It told him that in a distant Antiquity, 'the Egyptians and other peoples living near them maintained relations and dealings as far flung as we ourselves do and engaged in trading that the misfortunes of the world disrupted for thousands of years.' Like La Peyrère in the preceding century, Boulanger made use of Plato to demolish the biblical chronology that certain eminently respectable scholars, starting with the great Newton, were endeavouring to defend,[47] despite what they had read in Plato.

But let us indulge in a moment of comic relief and turn to an author slightly younger than Boulanger, Poinsinet de Sivry (1733–1804). Like so many others, he published a book on *Origins*.[48] It attracted a splendid passage of mockery from Grimm, who wrote as follows in his *Correspondance littéraire*:

> The late Monsieur Boulanger, to whom so many books have been attributed since his death and who was indeed the author of *L'Antiquité dévoilée*, pursued all his investigations into the universe through the medium of water and at every step discovered evidence of a flood. The author of the work that I am now discussing operated everywhere with fire and could take not a single step without discovering traces

of fire and its ravages. His perspicacity even extended to finding the word 'fire' in almost all the etymologies of geographical names. Could these gentlemen not have reached a compromise, the one making a little room for Monsieur Boulanger's water, the latter warming his water by means of the former gentleman's fire? The result might have been a rarefaction of the air that we could use to good effect.

That would certainly have constituted a return to sources, for the Ancients delighted in playing with water and fire.

The immense curiosity that possessed Nicolas Boulanger was that of a dilettante. Giuseppe Bartoli, who was a professor of Greek and Italian literature at the University of Turin and 'antiquarian' to the king of Sardinia, was more like what we would call a professional. By this I mean that he read Plato in the original Greek, was informed about Greek history by sources that were instructive on the period, and also that he was as able as the next man to relate the ancient text to the present, for he wrote an explanation to accompany his French translation (embellished with passages of Italian verse) of the speech made by King Gustavus III of Sweden at the opening of the 1778 Diet. Bartoli met Edward Gibbon in 1764. Gibbon judged him to be 'a bit of a charlatan but very learned' and, in truth, capable of spreading 'a great deal of enlightenment' through the study of both texts and monuments. Bartoli was certainly a bit mad, but it was a madness that he shared with many of his contemporaries: like the French orientalist De Guignes, he believed that Chinese characters and the Egyptian hieroglyphs denoted one and the same language.[49]

Let us now examine his remarkable book. It was published in Stockholm in 1779 and was entitled *Discours par lequel Sa Majesté le roi de Suède a fait l'ouverture de la Diète, en suédois, traduit en français et en vers italiens, avec un essai sur l'explication historique que Platon a donnée à son Atlantide et qu'on a pas considérée jusqu'à présent* ... (The speech with which His Majesty the king of Sweden opened the Diet, in Swedish, translated into French and into Italian verse, together with an essay on the historical explanation that Plato gave of his Atlantis, which has, until now, not been taken into consideration ...). Why Sweden? There was no question of a return to Rudbeck, with whose work Bartoli was familiar and whom he severely criticized right from the start of his essay. Sweden was unquestionably part of Enlightenment Europe. Germaine Necker, who had almost married Gibbon, eventually married Monsieur de Staël, the Swedish ambassador to Paris. Gustavus III was a typical example of an enlightened despot and was believed to operate as an agent for Paris. In 1772 he organized a *coup d'état*. He was a reformer, for he gave freedom to both foreigners and Jews. Voltaire had praised him and copious evidence testifies to the interchange of ideas between Stockholm and other European capitals.[50] He was also the hero of a drama by Scribe that would have made a fine libretto for Verdi's *Masked Ball*.

The key-word in the title of Bartoli's book is 'historical'. Bartoli was the first to see what nobody else had understood since the time of Plato: namely, that Atlantis was a mask for imperialist and maritime Athens. Here is what Bartoli says: 'Can our *philosophes* really continue to be deceived by the political submersion of the isle of Atlantis, that is to say this image of the decadence suffered by the republic of Athens, abandoned by all and crushed by the domination of its enemies?'[51] In other words, Bartoli had realized that behind the submersion of Atlantis we should detect the collapse of Athens, which had fallen into the hands of its enemies at the end of the Peloponnesian War, following decades of maritime imperialism. Better still, Bartoli had understood—perfectly understood—that the war between Athens and Atlantis was really a civil war within Athens itself: 'We should certainly agree that this disunity in the Republic of Athens, this sedition whose unfortunate effects, according to Plato, stemmed from the fact that within the State there were several States, was marvellously represented by the image of two separate countries at war.' Bartoli's central idea is that we should conclude from this representation that: 'It is all about one people, one town and one government that I am not yet sure whether to describe as all too well known or all too little known: namely the Athenians, always the Athenians, ever the Athenians'.[52]

Bartoli was well in advance of both his own century and the century that followed. Nobody took him seriously and many even ridiculed him. Thomas Henri-Martin, generally so lucid, was extremely severe: 'It is obvious that, in order to defend his theory, Bartoli had to make many mistranslations in his rendering of the texts upon which he relies.'[53] It is quite true that Bartoli sometimes slips from history into historicism. After all, the *Republic* is not, as he believes, a history of Athens. But in the last analysis, of all the commentators that we have passed in review, he is virtually the only one to understand that the myth that Plato created called for a *political* interpretation and that, in order to understand the myth, you need first to read Thucydides.

At the end of this chapter on the Atlantis of the Enlightenment, I should point out that not everyone at the time took an interest in the myth that Plato had created. For example, neither Montesquieu nor Rousseau manifested the slightest interest in this imaginary continent. Furthermore, a man such as Athanasius-Hyacinth Anquetil-Duperron (1731–1805), who travelled in the West Indies and certainly took an interest in the debate about America, refers to the *Timaeus* only to cite the famous reminder to Solon proferred by the priest of Saïs: 'Solon, Solon, all you Greeks are eternal children.'[54] So he certainly could have mentioned it but did not reckon this to be a good opportunity to do so.

CHAPTER 5

THE GREAT TURNING-
POINT, 1786–1841

It is not easy to impose a rank order upon the intellectual world that I have tried to describe from the point of view of its versions of Atlantis. From our lofty historical vantage point, we are of course free to favour a 'rationalist' lineage of thought that we can trace back to the sixteenth century, with José de Acosta in Spain and, in France, Michel de Montaigne, who rejected the Atlantis craze and all the various 'nationalistic' forms that it took. Should we pick out a 'reasonable' or 'rationalist' tendency running all the way from what Paul Hazard, in a famous book, called *La Crise de conscience européenne* (The Crisis of European Consciousness), (which the author reckons to have started around 1670) right down to a bold university professor such as G. Bartoli? The question is certainly debatable. Of course, Voltaire is more representative of his age than the obscure Abbé Jacques-Julien Bonnaud who in 1786 published in The Hague (in a Protestant country) a book entitled *Hérodote, historien du people hébreu sans le savoir*,[1] supporting the theory that Atlantis was Palestine in disguise. All the same, a historian cannot proceed as though Abbé Bonnaud never existed.

It is true that, between 1787 and 1789, one publisher, Charles Garnier, published thirty-nine volumes of a series entitled *Voyages imaginaires, romantiques, merveilleux, allégoriques et critiques* (Imaginary, romantic, marvellous, allegorical and critical voyages) that started off with *Robinson Crusoe*. But the connection between this long series and the explosion of the 1789 Revolution is not clear, and the *Critias* did not figure in that anthology, although Lucian's *True Stories* did. To find an Atlantis before or during the revolutionary crisis, we must turn to a figure very different from both Abbé Bonnaud and Charles Garnier: Jean-Baptiste Isoard, better known by his pseudonym Delisle de Sales (1743–1816). In his youth he had been a protégé of Voltaire's and in his later years he himself became the protector of both Chateaubriand and the specialist in the occult, Fabre d'Olivet. Delisle de Sales was a founding member of the Institut de France and seems to have been unaffected by the least trace of an inferiority complex: the inscription (borrowed from Buffon) that he had engraved upon his bust read 'God, man, nature: he explained them all'.

From the start, Delisle de Sales was a representative of the Enlightenment, but with one characteristic that distinguished him from many of his contemporaries: he was resolutely opposed to persecutions of the Jews. To be sure, the Enlightenment paved the way for the emancipation of the Jews, but it required them to pay for it by abandoning everything that had for centuries distinguished them from their contemporaries. In 1777, Delisle de Sales, for his part, declared, 'The Jews are neither physical nor moral monsters: they should be pitied and enlightened, not exterminated ... A Jew is a human being before being a devotee of a particular religion and even before being a Jew.'[2]

Admittedly, Voltaire had written, 'All the same, they should not be burnt', but before venturing to proclaim this principle of tolerance, he had heaped upon them every imaginable insult. Delisle de Sales, who was half a century younger than Voltaire and an extremely mediocre writer, was an intermediary, one of the many writers who, from a distance, can be seen to have ensured the transitions between the Enlightenment and Romanticism. In 1779, Delisle de Sales embarked upon an immense compilation entitled *Histoire nouvelle de tous les peuples du monde ou Histoire des hommes* (A new history of all the peoples of the world or a history of mankind), a work of 52 volumes. This *Histoire des hommes* starts by picking an ironical and public quarrel with both Sacred History and mythology. When Abbé Bonnaud, who died in the massacres of September 1792, launched an attack in the name of God upon 'the historian of mankind', it was aimed at Delisle de Sales. De Sales operated perfectly openly. According to him, when the figures of mythology 'abandoned the stage, they were replaced by human beings who stepped forward to play before their fellows'. The history of the earliest times could not be confined to that of the Hebrew people, with which it had often been deliberately confused. 'Only one people has a recognized history that stretches back from one generation to another, all the way to the cradle of the world; and that is the Hebrew people. But the proof provided by its annals is of a superior order and an examination of its monuments does not figure in the plan for the present work.'[3] None of this is anything out of the ordinary and it all manifests the influence of Voltaire's *Candide*.

Delisle de Sales places the people of Atlantis at the heart of universal history, but is careful to add, with his customary irony, 'Clearly, all that I write about the people of Atlantis can be accommodated with Genesis. Were that not the case, this part of my work would have to be rejected, for the authority of Moses is everything and mine is nothing.' The history of the earliest times thus does concern the Atlantes, but Delisle de Sales is at pains not confuse those inhabitants of Atlantis with the people known to Plato. For Atlantis was at most a colony, whatever the writers imitating Fontenelle (in other words, partisans of a 'plurality of worlds', such as Bailly and Rudbeck) might say.[4] Still within the Enlightenment tradition, Delisles de Sales sets out to discover 'the very earliest people', which was 'certainly not the people of God'.[5] He suggests that the place to look for this people is the vast region of the Caucasus mountains stretching from Turkestan to the frozen sea.[6] 'The earliest people of the Caucasus may not have the advantage of going back in an uninterrupted line, generation by generation, to the period when human clay was imbued with life by the hand that tossed the world into space',[7] but it could claim the same huge advantage as the Athenians: it was an autochthonous people. Prometheus and Neptune were the heroes of a people that was autochthonous, quite the opposite of the biblical people, which, whether by choice or as a punishment, constituted the wandering people *par excellence*.[8]

It is always fascinating to observe an intellectual shift. With his notion of the Caucasus as the place of origins, Delisle de Sales is not all that far from what Léon Poliakov, in his book published in 1971, called *The Aryan Myth*. All that is lacking is for linguistics to tack on the kinship of Indo-European languages (or what German scholars preferred to call 'Indo-Germanic' languages). So in tune with his time was Delisle de Sales that, having blithely published a book entitled *Ma République: auteur Platon* (My Republic: author Plato) in 1791, the year of the king's flight to Varennes, in 1802 he brought out a *Mémoire en faveur de Dieu* (A memoir in favour of God), which appeared at the same time as the *Génie du Christianisme* written by his famous disciple, François-Auguste de Chateaubriand.

Delisle de Sales's immediate circle of friends included two very different figures: one was Chateaubriand, the author of *Atala*, *René* and *Les Martyrs*, who was so adept at merging the marvels of Homer with those of Christianity; the other was Fabre d'Olivet, the great master of the occult. Faced with this bizarre conjunction, it occurred to me that Chateaubriand, whose first book was an *Essai historique sur les Révolutions*, published in London in 1797, must surely at some point have evoked the historicizing mythology of Atlantis, if only to criticize it. I embarked upon a search and found what I was looking for in *Le Génie du Christianisme*. Meditating on the ruins that he had seen in America, which might constitute evidence of a pre-Indian past, Chateaubriand wrote:

Man is suspended in the present, in between two abysses: behind him and before him, all is dark ... But whatever the conjectures on these American ruins may be, when combined with the visions of a primitive world and the chimera of an Atlantis, for the civilized nation that may have driven a plough through the plain where the Iroquois now hunt bears, the time needed in order to accomplish its destiny was no longer than that which swallowed up the empires of the likes of Cyrus, Alexander and Caesar.[9]

Now let us turn to Fabre d'Olivet. Although a member of Delisle de Sales's social circle, he was considerably younger than de Sales. He was born in 1767 and died in 1825 and was a contemporary of Chateaubriand and Napoleon. He was without doubt the founder of France's occultist religion, known by its initiates simply as 'the Tradition'. Let us borrow the portrait of him by Pierre Leroux, the inventor of the word 'socialism' and a close friend of George Sand, whose disciples—and there were many of them—called him Piotr the Red. This is how he describes Fabre around 1857, in his weighty book *La Grève de Samarez* (The Samarez Strike):

A great mind lost in the dreams of the occult sciences and the mysteries of alchemy, and over-inclined to wrap himself in clouds of esotericism. In the middle of an ideally liberated world, he was determined to reconstruct a secret temple. He appointed himself its priest in the ancient manner, intermingling Egyptian beliefs with Christianity.[10]

His biography is obscure on a number of points: for instance, we know nothing of his possible relations with dissident Jews.[11]

Fabre d'Olivet did not intend his oeuvre to be either mystical in the manner of *Illuminati* such as Saint-Martin or artistic in the manner of Chateaubriand, whom Sainte-Beuve famously described as 'an Epicurean with a Catholic imagination'. Rather, he saw himself as a scholar, representing 'knowledge revealed at the dawn of the ages',[12] knowledge that was held solely by its 'imperial theosophist'.

In other words, he promulgated a gnosticism that owed much to the Enlightenment tradition, but in particular developed whatever he had found in Delisle de Sales, imparting to it an extravagant and baroque luxuriance.

As early as 1797, the Atlantis theme appeared in Fabre's writing. A passage in *L'Invisible journal politique, littéraire et moral*, no. 7, dated 26 May 1797, runs as follows: 'Who knows whether the Atlantes [*Athlantes (sic)* in the French] were not privileged to return [*reçevoir*, a misprint for *revenir* in the French][13] more than once from the ice of winter to nature's springtime?' Fabre d'Olivet created a genre of writing very similar to that of modern science fiction, as indeed did Plato, although Fabre did not take as much care to make his story believable as Plato did. A twentieth-century example of writing in a similar genre might be that of Isaac Asimov, the author of the masterpiece, *Foundation*.

Fabre's imaginary world, like any other, naturally feeds upon reality, 'reality' in his case being provided by his reading: Rudbeck, Bailly, Buffon and Boulanger and, of course, Delisle de Sales, his immediate teacher. The Jews and the Atlantes are certainly the principal players in this theosophist's historical novels; or, to put it another way, Atlantis, along with his own reflections on Hebrew history, constituted Fabre d'Olivier's obsessive theme. That may not seem particularly surprising to anyone who has been following my account so far, but although the ingredients may seem familiar, the way they are put together is quite different.[14] For the sake of brevity, let us call this syncretism, bearing in mind, however, that this was a syncretism that was adapted to the spirit of the age and was accompanied by all the required sycophantic dedications to powerful figures of the day. Were Fabre's Jews really Jews? In their way, they were the 'vanished people' of Bailly and Court de Gébelin's *Le Monde primitif*. In 1815, Fabre published a book entitled *La Langue hébraïque restituée* in which, without the slightest hesitation, he 'demonstrated' that the real meaning of Hebrew words had been lost ever since the captivity in Babylon. As he saw it, it was up to him to re-establish that meaning and show that Hebrew was identical to Egyptian—a task that was made considerably easier by the fact that Champollion had not yet decoded the Egyptian hieroglyphs. Fabre pushed his demonstration close to the limit, producing a translation of the beginning of Genesis that was totally at odds with the traditionally accepted meaning.

The interplay between the Hebrews and the Atlantes figures in the *Lettres à Sophie* as well as in the *Histoire du genre humain*. It is hard to summarize Fabre's sometimes astonishing plots, so let me simply set out a few examples in order to demonstrate that, right from the start, in Fabre's first book, *Lettres à Sophie*, the biblical story was deeply interwoven with the Platonic framework, even more so than in the works of Cosmas Indicopleustes. Adam (Adim) is twenty years of age. He is the son of Eloim, Neptune's high priest, and is the most accomplished of all the inhabitants of Atlantis. Eve (Evenha), with whom he is in love, is the priestess of Venus.[15] Their love affair runs into trouble and only reaches its desired climax after the flood that was to swallow up Atlantis (one of many, according to Boulanger's cosmology).[16] The couple then find themselves in the Caucasus mountains.

When dealing with primitive times, Fabre divides the most ancient people known into three groups that correspond well enough to the three functions identified by Georges Dumézil: the Atlantes are the inventors of agriculture, the Peris (Persians?) are the inventors of religions; and the Scythians are the inventors of warfare. The first group corresponds to the Gods, the second to the Genies, the third to the Giants. Later, following a series of complicated events, the Hebrews become the heirs to the Atlantes, the Chinese become the heirs to the Peris, and the Celts become the heirs to the Scythians, but all this happens after 'an upheaval similar to that which destroyed Atlantis'.[17] However, the future does not belong to peoples of thoroughbred stock. The Atlantes interbreed with the

Peris, to produce the trading peoples; unions between the Scythians and the Peris produce the Medes, Aryans and so on. We are by now truly poles apart from Atlanto-nationalism as created by Rudbeck and, before him, by the Spanish theorists at the time of the great discoveries and the empire of Charles V.

L'Histoire du genre humain presents a different scenario, in which a more important role is assigned to the mythology of India, to which *Les Lettres à Sophie* made no more than a passing allusion. Apart from that, however, the message is identical. The object is to bring together 'the sacred books of all nations', including the Bible, without favouring 'an ignorant and poor small country called Judaea', but certainly not ignoring the Bible, since Fabre himself— and he alone—holds the only true key to it.[18] Much of this book is devoted to a gigantic conflict between 'the White Race' and 'the Black Race', the latter being the more ancient, which, in ancient times, 'dominated the earth and held the sceptre of power there'.

At this point, the great masters Rudbeck and Bailly make an appearance, for Fabre certainly acknowledges his debt to them:

> The vague memory of the [Nordic] origin [of the White Race] made the north pole the nursery of the human race ... It gave rise to ... the many traditions that led Olaus Rudbeck to place Plato's Atlantis in Scandinavia and authorized Bailly to discern the cradle of all the earth's sciences, arts and mythologies on the deserted rocks whitened by the frosts of Spitzbergen.

In a footnote, Fabre at this point adds: 'In the writings of these two authors one may read the many testimonies with which they support their assertions. They are inadequate for their hypotheses as a whole. But they become irresistible in determining where the White Race first lived and its place of origin.'[19]

Fabre nevertheless has no qualms about shifting the location of Atlantis, in contradiction to the two predecessors he has just named. The North is the home of the White race, which will become the

Celtic or Scythian race; in the South live the Black race, to which the Atlantes, 'that is to say the masters of the universe', belong.[20] The contrast between the two groups is not just a matter of warrior prowess. The Celts, guided by their druids, vanquish the Atlantes, but it is through contact with them that they acquire 'a vague knowledge of writing'. The Atlantes, like the Arabs, the Phoenicians and the Hebrews, write from right to left. The Celts reverse this because where they live the trajectory of the sun passes in the opposite direction to that known by the Atlantes ..., who live in the southern hemisphere.[21] Our ancestors, the Gauls, thus introduced the habit of writing from left to right; and since the Celts incorporated Rudbeck's Goths, their earliest characters were 'runes'.

The Atlantes lived by 'the dogma of one sole principle',[22] in other words monotheism, which they had taken over from the Hebrews. As in *Les Lettres à Sophie*, certain mixed races were by no means the least glorious. The Arabs, for example, were an ancient mixture of Celts and Atlantes. As for the Indian civilization, it had adopted 'the calendar of the Atlantic peoples'.[23] Each of the 'revolutions' that punctuated the onward march of history (for which Fabre created a system parallel to that devised by his contemporary Chateaubriand) was marked by borrowings such as these.

However, the crucial centre for decisive fusions and mutations was Egypt. Of course, Fabre d'Olivet's fables about Egypt were not at all innovative. Antiquity already had its own 'Egyptian image', as Herodotus was one of the first to testify, and also its 'Egypt of astrologers',[24] and travellers had been marvelling at Egypt's wonders right up to the time of Bonaparte's expedition, which liberated an almost unprecedented fund of new information. Meanwhile, in the eighteenth century the myth had been given new life, as is shown by, for example, the libretto of *The Magic Flute*.

'We should not forget that Egypt was the last country to remain under Atlantan domination', wrote Fabre d'Olivet, with his usual priceless solemnity. Atlantis had been born from a largely imaginary journey in Egypt, and it was now there, in Fabre d'Olivet's work, that it died. According to Fabre, Egypt was located at the crossroads of two traditions, that of the 'Southern Race' and that of the 'Northern Race', which had later imposed upon the former its own northern religion and laws.

> Through the former tradition, it even went back to an earlier tradition and preserved some idea of the 'Austral' race that had preceded the 'southern one'. That first race, from which the primitive name Atlantis may have come, had totally perished in a terrible flood which, covering the earth, had ravaged it from one pole to the other and had submerged the immense and magnificent island that this race inhabited, beyond the seas.[25]

That race was the Red race and, as Fabre made clear, Atlantis was America, but an America far vaster than the one we know: 'It extended much further southward toward the South Pole.'[26] Fabre then proceeded to borrow from Plato, the Plato of the *Timaeus*, the *Critias* and Book III of the *Laws*, the description of what happens in times of flooding: only those who live in the mountains survive. The Egyptian priesthood, which was known to Fabre more through Plato than through Herodotus and was master of these traditions, was thus provided with a further opportunity to call the Greeks 'eternal children'.[27]

Moses grew up in Egypt but, after killing an Egyptian (as Exodus 2. 11–14 recounts), he moved to Ethiopia. 'It was there that he encountered an expatriate Arab (or Celto-Atlantan) people, the Hebrews, whose priest he became. His father-in-law Jethro in all likelihood even passed on to him 'a few genethliacal books relating to the Atlantes'.[28] History had come full circle and now Moses, along with the Greek Orpheus and the Hindu Foë (Fabre's name for Buddha), could become one of the three great reformers of his age. 'Moses' sole mission had been to preserve cosmogonic principles of every kind [which, Fabre explained, constituted 'the most ancient tradition on earth', even older than the Atlantes] and to store away the seeds of all future institutions, as it were in a holy ark. The people to which he entrusted the care of this ark was uncouth, but robust, made the stronger by its exclusive laws.'[29]

Fabre's Atlantis was not Judaea but nor was it an anti-Judaea. It was the source of all that the Jews, Celto-Atlantes, and other peoples too, such as the Mohammedan Arabs[30] (whose tradition was of greater purity) have—somewhat despite themselves—passed down to us. Thus do we 'to some extent owe our very existence to the disaster of Atlantis',[31] ('we' being the White or 'northern' race). For it was thanks to that disaster that our own continent emerged from the waters.

Fabre d'Olivet owed a great deal to his own imagination but among his debts of gratitude to others there was one that he acknowledged so precisely that one wonders whether he was not acquainted with the unpublished manuscript of Boulanger mentioned above. Fabre writes as follows:

> Boulanger, who undertook much research on this subject, believes with reason that after the loss of Atlantis, the peoples of our hemisphere who survived remained stupefied and continued for a long time to wander, without daring to settle; he believes that this life of savages grew out of the terror that that event had impressed upon them.[32]

That is remarkably accurate summary of the theories of the man who believed so steadfastly in a great succession of floods.

Why have I dwelt at such length upon Fabre d'Olivet? There can clearly be no doubt that his whole account is imaginary. But whether he was conscious of the entirely fictional nature of what can hardly be called a theory remains uncertain. He was a contemporary of German Romantic poets such as Novalis who, in his *Heinrich von Ofterdingen*,[33] described Atlantis as a place of ideal beauty.

What is interesting and novel in Fabre d'Olivet is the fact that his great fantasy is carefully set within a time-frame, unsupported by any historical source of course but nevertheless presented as a partly biblical, partly neo-pagan reconstruction of the history of humanity. Within a few decades, Thomas-Henri Martin, a disciple of Victor Cousin, the official philosopher of the July Monarchy,[34] was to banish all Atlantis enthusiasts to the realm of the imagination, yet after no more than a few further decades, certain so-called scholars would, in their turn, once again be reconstructing an antediluvian world, albeit without creating as many priestly or kingly individuals as Fabre d'Olivet. In other words, at the dawn of Romanticism, the young 1789 patriot who, according to Léon Cellier, Fabre d'Olivet had been, who had first begun to speak of Atlantis at the time of the Directory, had two ways of looking at things: one that came from the Enlightenment and another that was capable of constructing a monstrous world set in an entirely fictional history.

Now let us take a look at one or two of Fabre d'Olivet's contemporaries in Italy and the kingdom of Great Britain and Ireland.

However forcefully Vico, in *La Scienza nova* had rejected everything that smacked of Rudbeck's Atlanto-nationalism, even in Italy he had been preaching largely in the desert. It has to be said that, as we have seen in connection with Count Gian Rinaldo Carli, Italy, with its past of Latin, Italic, Greek and Etruscan peoples, provided a prime terrain for the kinds of speculation that I am trying to analyse. At the beginning of the nineteenth century, Plato made a comeback in the works of Vincenzo Cuoco (1770–1823), a writer who for many years remained in obscurity but was the author of a *Platone in Italia*.[35] However, it was Angelo Mazzoldi who, in a book that appeared in Milan in 1840, that is to say shortly before the publication of Thomas-Henri Martin's destructive dissertation, carved out a place for Atlantis in the Italians' own history. His book bears one of those interminable titles favoured by ancient scholars and sometimes also by modern ones: *Dalle origini italiane e della diffusione dell'incivilimento italiano alla Fenicia, alla Grecia, e a tutte le nazioni asiatiche poste sul Mediterraneo* (On the Italian origins and the diffusion of Italian civilization to Phoenicia, Greece and all the Asiatic nations bordering the Mediterranean).[36] Here, many years after the Renaissance, we again find Plato as the master of a particular nationalism that is characterized by the fundamental feature of all nationalisms: all tend to seize hold of the most distant past the better to impose themselves in the present. In this respect, this work represents a regression from Fabre d'Olivet's great fantasy.

I believe that the nationalist myth of Atlantis exists in two British versions and one Irish one. All three are relatively late and stem from the occult and pre-Romantic tradition rather than from Enlightenment philosophy. So they fit perfectly into the great turning-point that I am endeavouring to analyse.

William Blake (1757–1827) was, give or take roughly a decade, a contemporary of Fabre d'Olivet. In his mythology, Albion, the ancestor of the Britons and 'the patriarch of the Atlantic continent', is a hero whose history 'precedes that of the Hebrews'. It goes back even beyond the fundamental principle that Blake (venturing rather further than Vico) lays down as follows: 'The Antiquity of every Nation under Heaven is no less sacred than that of the Jews.'[37] It would appear that this theme, which first appears in Blake's work in 1793, in the poem entitled *America*, was for him a fundamental one. In his poem *Jerusalem* (1804), Blake tells the Jews that their ancestors' origin came from Abraham, Heber, Sem, and Noah, who were druids.[38] Albion's England, heir—along with America—to Atlantis, is yet another homeland of the twelve tribes of Israel.[39]

Blake's oeuvre presents a strange mixture. In addition to the Platonic story, it included biblical tradition, fables about America, Celtic myth (much in vogue in Blake's day—that is to say soon after the triumphs of the pseudo-Ossian, the entirely fabricated bard created by Macpherson). 'Above Albion's land was seen the heavenly Canaan'[40] was a clear expression of the theme of national messianism. Captain F. Wilford, an Indianist and a contemporary of Blake's, tried out a quite different approach. He pooled whatever he could find in Marcellus (a figure who, as I mentioned in Chapter 2, is known to us only through Proclus's *Commentary on the Timaeus*[41]) with what he had learned from the Puranas (which mention distant, white, western islands, the *çreta dvîpa*). Then, after considering a number of other hypotheses, he eventually comes to the conclusion that the 'white isles' were at once Great Britain, as seen from India, and Atlantis; after which, he remarks with candour: 'Even if I find that I am correct, I am conscious of the fact that Great Britain could derive from this no new lustre greater than that which it already possesses.'[42]

At least the wisdom of India, so often at work throughout the Age of Enlightenment, thus came to bestow the finishing touches upon the antiquity and power of the island that ruled both India and the waves, for the thesis prefigured the formation of the British Empire. Thus, the Atlantes' conquest in a way provided an admirable balance in human history.

However, that same empire had enemies close to home in its neighbour, Ireland, which was constantly in revolt; and Captain Wilford himself had a highly cultivated rival in the person of Henry O'Brien. In 1834, the latter published, in both London and Dublin, a book entitled *The Round Towers of Ireland*. In 1976, a contemporary New York publisher reprinted this work under the much more intriguing title of *Atlantis in Ireland*. The difficulty is that neither the *Timaeus* nor the *Critias* are cited in this work in which the very name Atlantis never appears at all. The book's essential purpose was to draw attention to what was in those days a characteristic feature of the Irish landscape: namely the presence of its round, medieval-looking towers, which the author took to be the equivalent of the pyramids of Egypt.

This book presents Buddhism as the religion of the earliest human beings: Eve was a Buddhist. Ireland was a colony of Iran. And as for those towers, they were phallic in shape and so could be associated with the *lingams* of India. O'Brien was familiar with the works of a few of his predecessors: he cites both Bailly and Boulanger; but what can one make of a man who considers Tubalcain, the son of Abel's brother and the father of a line of blacksmiths, to be the equivalent of the Greek (*sic*) god Vulcan? Many years ago, one of my former students, Richard Gordon, presented me with this book as a gift. It does not appear to have been included in any current bibliography of Atlantis. Yet it is, albeit in a very different genre, just as imaginative as the works of Fabre d'Olivet. It criticizes Herodotus, not because— as Father Bonnaud was so shocked to find—he never mentioned the Jewish people, but because he does not speak of the round towers of Ireland—clearly an unforgivable crime. The modern editor of this work, Paul M. Allen, regards O'Brien as a precursor of Ignatius Donnelly, a writer whom we shall shortly be encountering.[43]

As we have noted, in 1841 Thomas-Henri Martin sounded the death-knell for Atlantomania in an appendix to his famous *Etudes sur le Timée de Platon*. But ten years earlier, in 1831, some hesitant pages had been written on this subject by a major scholar, Jean-Antoine Letronne (1787–1848). Letronne was one of the fathers of the modern science of Greek epigraphy and *the* father of that same science in its application to Graeco-Roman Egypt. To be sure, he reckoned that the story of Atlantis was simply a fable, but he thought that it had truly come from Egypt. The passion for Egypt of this contemporary of Champollion had, for once, overcome his critical acumen.[44]

CHAPTER 6

SOCIETIES THAT ARE OPEN AND THOSE THAT ARE CLOSED

C hapters 3, 4 and 5 of this book sketch in a description of 'national' versions of Atlantis, particularly in Spain, Sweden and Italy. Rudbeck's ideas marked Sweden so deeply that, as late as the twentieth century, it still harboured 'Rudbeckian Youth Groups' which, Jesper Svenbro tells me, were one manifestation of far-right tendencies. Italy produced no such phenomenon, nor—I think—did Spain. Certainly, the theories of Count Carli and Angelo Mazzoldi do not seem to have shaken Italy unduly.

And what of France? Very early on, it too produced ideologues and creators of national myths, in particular the Trojan legend out of which Ronsard, in his *Franciade*, tried to produce an epic. But Ronsard was already more of a writer than a creator of myths and ideologies, and *La Franciade* was a flop. Ronsard never proceeded beyond book IV in this bold project that was certainly a kind of national apologia, but of a literary rather than a myth-creating nature.

So was France spared this specific malady? On the whole the answer to that question is 'Yes', and the explanation is simple enough. After the *great* king, Louis XIV, came the *great* nation and then the *great* emperor. France was sufficient unto itself and, if its ideologues did need to resort to discourse on origins, the Gauls, Romans, Trojans and Franks provided all the material necessary. The one exception that proved the rule was a work by a native of Avignon, Fortia d'Urban, who in 1808 published a dissertation that endeavoured to show that an ancient people composed of Celts and Iberians had brought the civilization of Atlantis from Spain to France.[1] However, this amounted at most to an instance of a provincial, Occitan version of Atlantis that was of very little significance.

Far more interesting is a now forgotten work by Népomucène Lemercier (1771–1840). He was a member of the Académie française, where he was succeeded by Victor Hugo, no less, who, when taking over this chair, once occupied by Corneille, delivered a measured tribute to his immediate predecessor. Lemercier belonged to the intriguing generation that effected the transition from the Enlightenment to Romanticism. His father was secretary to the Duchesse de Lamballe, a friend and confidante of Queen Marie-Antoinette, and this aristocratic court lady was his godmother. He knew Bonaparte but refused to swear loyalty to the Emperor; and when the Bourbons returned, he continued to keep his distance.[2]

The work that interests me is entitled *L'Atlantiade ou la théogonie newtonienne*, a poem in six cantos published in Paris in 1812 and dedicated to the glory of Newton. According to its date of publication, *L'Atlantiade* constituted the last section of a large work 'divided into four parts devoted to the major generalities of the sciences, legislation, poetry and warfare'. Structurally, however, it appears as the first section of the work that Népomucène Lemercier started publishing in 1800, aspiring to be a Lucretius or a Francis Bacon rather than a modern Hesiod.

Long ago, this island of Atlantis had been called Eugaia or the Good Land. It was invaded by Atlas, who seems to share a number of characteristics with Napoleon. Before its invasion it had been inhabited by *Sumphytes*, that is to say human beings who lived according to the order of nature. Eugaia can probably be identified with the Europe laid waste by Napoleon's wars. Lemercier's purpose in this epic poem, the action of which unfolds 'in the Tropics', is 'to set out the general system of our sciences or at least of things discovered recently that as yet have no existence or names in poetry and the abstract names of which, constantly changing as new discoveries call for new words, could not be expressed in verse by any equivalent terms'.[3]

After ferocious fighting, Atlas is eventually defeated. But the ocean floods the foundations of his palace and submerges the island. A doctor named Zoophilos, the lover of Bione, saves whatever can be salvaged. Guided by him, the little group of survivors reaches the coast of America where peaceful Indians lead an idyllic life alongside the likes of Franklin and Vashington (sic), who were soon to set up a society based on science and reason. I need not pursue the analysis of this rather amazing text in which 'Sulphydre' (a nymph with a body composed of inflammable gas) is abandoned by her lover Pyrotonne (Thunder) who is, so to speak, inflamed by desire for Electrone. Let me cite just four lines from canto VI, in which Ocean declares: 'The fate of Atlantis and its black victors/ Will make you Europeans shudder./ Its engulfment, extending my domain,/ Will check the audacity of your future ventures'.[4] ('Le sort de l'Atlantide et de ses noirs vainqueurs/ De vos Européens fera frémir les coeurs;/ Son engloutissement qui grandit ma surface/De leurs trajets futurs arrêtera l'audace').

One year after the death of Népomucène Lemercier, Thomas-Henri Martin fancied he had brought to a close the ambiguous relations between Atlantis and the historical, geographical and cosmological sciences. Positivism may not have halted the fantasies of Atlantomania, but there can be no doubt that it did encourage a shift from mythologizing to novel-writing.

Our next witness is Jules Verne (1828–1905), the ace novelist of scientific adventures. So representative of the Atlantis of novels does he seem not only in France but worldwide that when the English researcher Paul Jordan was looking for an introductory citation for his book *The Atlantis Syndrome* (2001),[5] he decided he could do no better than pick the scene in which the heroes of *Twenty Thousand Leagues under the Sea*, Captain Nemo and Professor Arronax, his enforced guest, explore the ruins of the capital city of Atlantis, 450 nautical miles off the Atlantic coast of Morocco. The text is a famous one and shows that Jules Verne was well abreast of all the existing literature on Atlantis and was well informed about both those who believed the legend and those who called it a fable. Let me simply note, first, that Captain Nemo, an Indian prince at war with the British (the Cipayes revolt of Indians serving in the British army occurred in 1857) manifests no hostility at all toward the Germanic world; and secondly, that two out of three of the heroes of Verne's *Voyage to the Centre of the Earth* are Germans who are extremely sympathetic.

The 1870–71 war was soon to change all that. In *The Five Hundred Millions of the Begum* (1879) the hostile figure of the German made its appearance very much in the guise that it was to retain for several generations.

Here is a rapid summary of the plot of this story. Two men, one French, Doctor Sarrasin, the other German, Professor Schultze, from the University of Iena, find themselves to be the sole co-heirs to a gigantic fortune left by the Begum, an Indian princess who had married a French adventurer. The two men use their inheritances in very different ways. The French doctor, a hygiene specialist, builds, in Oregon, then a virtually virgin territory, an ideal city in which all the rules of hygiene and masculine democracy are applied. This perfect city is called France-Ville. It is constructed by thousands of Chinese coolies who do not receive their wages until they leave (racism is to be deplored, of course, but there *are* limits …). Every citizen of an age to bear arms belongs to the militia responsible for defending the town. A few leagues away, Herr Schultze has built Stahlstadt, a town of steel, a kind of factory-cum-city that is a gigantic imitation of the Krupp factories. It produces and exports thousands of cannons.

A young Alsatian, Marcel Bruckmann, arrives in Stahlstadt, where he becomes Herr Schultze's favourite collaborator and discovers his secret plan: to make an enormous cannon capable of launching a shell to destroy France-Ville and thereby help to establish German supremacy. The project of course fails and the shell becomes a satellite of planet Earth. As for Herr Schultze, he ends up as he deserves, a victim of the explosion of one of his own shells. France-Ville takes over Stahlstadt, in which production is thereafter directed to completely different ends.

The model of the two cities, the one pacific and the other belligerent, is several thousand years old. It of course goes without saying that the peace-loving city has to be capable of defending itself. The same model is to be found represented on the Mesopotamian 'Ur Standard' (in the British Museum) (see Fig. 1, p. 5), on the shield of Achilles in book XVIII of the *Iliad*, and on fifteenth-century manuscripts depicting a belligerent England and a peace-loving France. It is also to be found in the Platonic opposition between the primitive Athens and Atlantis (with the obvious very important difference that ancient Athens is governed by professional soldiers).

I am struck by one detail that brings Atlantis irresistibly to mind. When Jules Verne wishes to evoke the heart of the city that is governed dictatorially by Herr Schultze, he writes as follows: 'The centre of the spider's web that Stahlstadt reproduced was the Bull's Tower, a Cyclopean type of construction that dominated all the neighbouring buildings.'[6] In the *Critias* (119d–120e), it is the sacrifice of a bull, followed by the consumption of wine mixed in a crater with a dollop of the beast's blood that sets the seal on the alliance of the ten kings of Atlantis. As we have seen, Jules Verne was certainly familiar with Plato's text. In my view, his description of the city of steel was probably inspired by it.

In 1877, a young priest, Jacint Verdaguer (1845–1902) produced an epic, *Atlantis*, written in Catalan.[7] Verdaguer was a contemporary of Frédéric Mistral, who gave this Catalan epic an enthusiastic reception.[8] It is such a shame that, whereas the Catalans managed to maintain and develop their language, despite all the efforts of the Occitan Félibrège group, Mistral and his friends failed.

It goes without saying that Verdaguer's *Atlantis* is a scholarly epic that has more in common with the *Iliad* and is a very far cry from the popular epics that Milman Parry and Albert Lord were to record in the twentieth-century former Yugoslavia. Verdaguer had read the geographers, in particular Elisée Reclus, a famous intellectual anarchist but also a distinguished scholar, who believed that Atlantis had once actually existed. Verdaguer's work in ten cantos was preceded by an introduction, followed by a conclusion, and in canto VII included a chorus composed of Greek islands. It relied heavily on classical mythology: its principal protagonist is Hercules, who abducts the nymph Hesperis from Atlantis, where she has produced twelve sons for Atlas, providing him with the children who would populate the Iberian peninsula; even Portugal, so often an enemy, is not overlooked. Hercules brings the orange tree to Baetica (Andalusia) and eventually founds not only Barcelona but also Hispalis (Seville). At the same time, however, he works for a god known sometimes as the Highest One (Altissimus), sometimes as Jehovah or Adonaï. In canto IX, the Atlantes try to climb up to heaven while the angel who watches over the great island reascends to it, crossing the path of the angel of Spain, who is descending to present the latter with world domination.

An old anchorite who has rescued a shipwrecked survivor off the coast of Portugal tells his story to a Genovese mariner who is none other than Christopher Columbus. Having saved the life of the future explorer and instructed him as to his mission, the old man announces at the end of the epic that he is now free to die. Atlantis was magnificent but also the duct that brought every vice into the world, in particular the prime sin, incest. In the tenth and last canto, the olive tree, alongside the orange tree, is designated as the tree of the Cross. To show that the nationalism of Verdaguer was of an open, rather than a tyrannical, nature, let me simply refer to line 263 of canto I. Earlier, when speaking of the Pyrenees that separate Spain from France, Verdaguer had initially used extremely pejorative terms: *L'enemiga França*, then the *envejosa França*, but in the end he settled for *La veïna França*; France was simply a neighbour, no longer an enemy, no longer jealous or arrogant. Manuel de Falla (1866–1946), not himself a Catalan, was at the end of his life to put the poem magnificently to music.

Naturally, Verlanguer was not alone in linking Atlantis to Spain either positively or negatively. In 1929, Victor Bérard invoked the existence of *corridas* to justify situating Atlantis, with its bull sacrifices, in southern Spain, and in 1939, Adolf Schulten merged Atlantis with Tartessos, at the mouth of the Guadalquivir.[9] It would seem that the passion for localization, which is sometimes—but not always—perfectly disinterested, has never disappeared.

In situating France-Ville and Stahlstadt in America, Jules Verne was echoing attempts characteristic of the time of the July Monarchy to found ideal cities for which America seemed a suitable location. One example is provided by Cabet's *Icarie*. Meanwhile, ever since 1830, the eve of the July Revolution, an altogether real French colonial empire had been developing in Africa. By the time of the Third Republic, it eventually comprised close on one third of the African continent, with the immense Sahara desert at its centre.

I am grateful to Chantal Foucrier for informing me that in 1868 D.A. Godron, a professor in the faculty of Sciences of Nancy University, published a series of lectures entitled *Atlantis and the Sahara*.[10] Having already read Pierre Benoit's *Atlantis*, I thought at first that the geographer Etienne-Félix Berlioux, who figures largely in the material about the Saharan Hoggar, was an imaginary figure. But in truth, within the framework of his teaching in the Faculty of Letters in Lyon, the real Professor E.-F. Berlioux developed an interest in the Moroccan Atlas Mountains and the Algerian Sahara.[11] In the early twentieth century, before Germany had succeeded in establishing colonies on a scale comparable to those of France, the ethnologist Leo Frobenius was also looking for Atlantis, which he duly found further to the south, close to Niger.[12]

In May 1881, the Treaty of Bardo created the French Protectorate of Tunisia. Jules Ferry was not seeking an Atlantis there, but the French Ministry of Education, following the model provided by the scholars who had accompanied Bonaparte to Egypt, nevertheless published an *Exploration scientifique de la Tunisie*, in which my friend Hervé Duchêne discovered a 'Note on Atlantis'.[13] Its author, Charles Tissot, a diplomat whom the young Saloman Reinach served in the capacity of a 'ghost writer', cites an extensive body of literature, most of it in French, and expresses the belief that the continent really had existed (as was the opinion, as late as 1913, of Pierre Termier, a well-known geologist[14]). Tissot concludes his brief enquiry as follows:

> If one accepts, along with the geologists, that in the past, to the west of Spain, there must have existed a vast continent of which the Canaries and the Azores may be considered to be the remnants, then there is no reason to continue to doubt that that great land was the point of departure for many migrations. The movement eastward of its peoples must thus have constituted the earliest foreign invasion of Africa that is still remembered.

(Of course, it was to be by no means the last!)

In the eighteenth century, the couple Athens–Sparta had functioned as rival models in France and in Germany and also in the mythology of French–German relations. Was it the case that now there was a similar rivalry between France and Germany surrounding Atlantis or the Athens–Atlantis pair? The answer has to be 'No'. In twentieth-century France, Atlantis figured essentially in novels such as *L'Atlantide* (1919), by Pierre Benoit (1886–1962)[15] and in others too that enjoyed less success. More recently, it also became the subject of strip-cartoons such as those produced by Edgar P.

Jacobs.[16] Comprehensive theoretical works were rare, that of Pierre Termier, cited above, being an exception. At the level of scholarly works, France's contribution in the first half of the century consisted of a little book by Paul Couissin (the author of pioneering works on the Greek Sceptics), entitled *L'Atlantide de Platon et les origines de la civilisation*,[17] which calmly set out to destroy the legend. As far as I know, no attempts were made to identify Atlantis with France.

The Atlantis of Pierre Benoit's novel, situated in the Hoggar, is an anti-world, if only because it is presented as a gynaecocracy. The Hoggar in general is governed by women, and the domain of Antinea belongs to a female religious diviner who lures a series of lovers, several of whom are French army officers, to their deaths, then embalms them and deposits their bodies in niches in a 'red marble hall'. Interestingly enough, the only scholarly journal dealing with the Sahara that is mentioned in the novel is a German geological review,[18] the *Zeitschrift für Erdkunde in Berlin*. To emphasize the deeply pagan character of the Hoggar Atlantis, with its Egyptian veneer of shoddy goods and its 'Hiram-king', a leopard that bears the name of a Phoenician mentioned in the Bible, the novelist amuses himself, as is his right, by making one of his heroes, Captain Morhange (eventually killed by the other hero, Lieutenant de Saint-Avit) a contributor to the *Atlas of Christianity*, which is published by an erudite Benedictine monk, Dom Granger, whose name, in an only slightly different form, is that of a nineteenth-century monk, Dom Guéranger.

Pierre Benoit's *Atlantis* is certainly not France, and its queen is more like the daughter of a Parisian tart and a Polish count than a descendant of Poseidon-Neptune. The novelist does nothing to dispel the ambiguity, for he equips the palace of Antinea with a complete copy of Plato's *Critias*; however, that is surely well within the novelist's licence. France did produce other 'Atlantis' novels besides that of Paul Benoit, but they have elicited murmurs of 'bankrupt novel-writing',[19] so let us move on without more ado.

The situation in Germany was quite different, not that there were no novels about Atlantis in Germany, but precisely because the most famous of them, *Die Letzte Koenigin von Atlantis* (The Last Queen of Atlantis), was inspired by National–Socialist ideology. Meanwhile, in contrast, Gerhart Hauptmann's novel entitled *Atlantis*, published in 1912, was deeply critical of German society.[20]

It was mainly in the wake of the 1918 disaster that the Atlantis theme was developed, taking forms that were in many cases ostensibly scholarly but failed to mask the fact that their contents were essentially ideological. It is not surprising that pre-Nazi and Nazi ideology seized on the theme with an alacrity which, with hindsight, justifies the Jules Verne of *The Begum's Five Hundred Millions*; what is surprising, though, is that the collapse of 1945 did so little to check this sort of madness. Here are four examples.

The first is a book by Karl Georg Zschaetzsch, *Atlantis, the Original Homeland of the Aryans*.[21] To judge by the map that served as an illustration to the book (see Fig. 18, p. 123), this Atlantis was of a relatively modest size, about the same area as Spain, and was situated off the coasts of Spain and Morocco. Blithely combining Plato, Jordanes and the *Edda*, in the manner of Rudbeck but without citing him, he calmly explains that when the historian of the Goths (Jordanes) calls the Scandinavian peninsula the *vagina gentium*, what he is referring to is Atlantis, which is the true native land of the Goths. The Franks too were of Atlantan origin, as were the Saxons who populated Great Britain. Zschaetzsch's broad-mindedness even extends to finding traces of Atlantis in the traditions of the Incas of Peru. Heracles, Indra, Thor and Inti-Kapak are just a few of his heroes of Atlantan origin. Let me simply cite what appears to be the key pronouncement in this little book: 'Ohne arische Grundsätze kann eben kein Staat Gestehen':[22] 'Without Aryan principles, no State can exist'.

The second work that I must mention is Albert Herrmann's *Unsere Ahnen und Atlantis*[23] (Our ancestors and Atlantis). The sub-title translates as 'The maritime empire of the men of the North, from

Scandinavia to North Africa'. The author knew of Zschaetzsch, to whom he devotes an ironical comment on page 17, declaring himself unable to follow him in 'his perilous leap into the Atlantic Ocean'; for his part, he will stick to reality. And who was this Albert Herrmann? A professor at the University of Berlin, no less, an avowed Nazi who became more or less the 'Führer' of the German press. The territories that his enquiry covers extend as far away as Tunisia. One of the colleagues whom he acknowledges at the beginning of his book is Professor Poinssot, the Director of Antiquities in what was then the French Protectorate of Tunisia. In his foreword (p. 5), Hermann explains that his compatriots now have before them a new ideal that comes not from abroad but from the blood and soil (*Blut und Boden*) of Germany itself. It was the introduction of Christianity that encouraged the belief that the Germanic peoples were barbarians. This enquiry of his shows that, on the contrary, their lands had enjoyed a golden age in the second millennium before the Christian era and even prior to the flowering of the Mycenaean civilization.

What is the documentary basis upon which this thesis rests? It is *The Chronicle of Ura-Linda*, more's the pity. This is a 'marvellous' manuscript discovered in 1867 by the librarian and archivist of the Helder region, in the Dutch province of Frisia—a treasure claimed to have been passed down from generation to generation. Unfortunately, this miraculous chronicle was more or less universally recognized as a forgery, as Albert Herrmann was perfectly well aware—not that this deterred him from endeavouring, with the aid of a Dutch National–Socialist, Herrmann Wirth, to salvage from it anything that was salvageable: a difficult project given that a number of very recent texts had found their way into the ancient chronicle, Volney's *Les Ruines* (1791), for one.[24]

Herrmann reconstructed a Germanic empire whose material traces took the form of 'Megaliths' (Carnac, Stonehenge, etc.), an idea that was subsequently taken up by many of his successors.[25] But above all the *Chronicle of Ura-Linda* provided him with the names of three

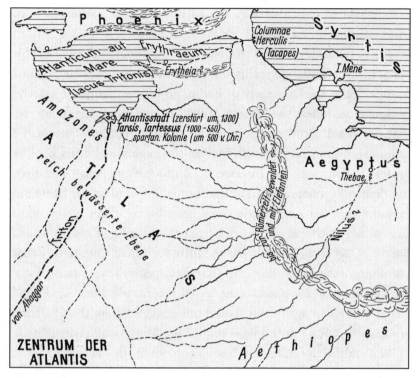

17. Map showing the position of Atlantis according to Albert Herrmann, *Katastrophen, Naturgewalten und Menschenschicksale*. G. Schönfeld, Berlin, 1936.

primordial 'mothers', Frya, Lyda and Finda. Frya (also spelt Freya) came from Germanic legend. Lyda was black, Finda brown. The great Atlanto-Germanic empire disappeared in 1680 BC. But the peoples of the North did not disappear. They are even to be found in the *Iliad* and the *Odyssey*.[26] The fact that it was Poseidon who built Troy proves that it was certainly an Atlantan town. As for the *Odyssey*, the land of the Phaeacians was clearly located in Tunisia (pp. 144–50). How could these deductions be reconciled with a Germanic Atlantis? Only with difficulty, obviously, but there was, after all, a temple of Poseidon in Phaeacia and that was quite enough to reassure

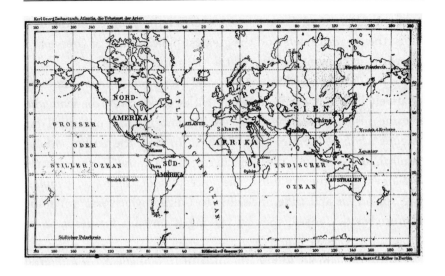

18. Map and title page from the work by Karl Georg Zschaetzsch, *Atlantis die Urheimat der Arier* (Atlantis, the Original Homeland of the Aryans), Arier-Verlag, Berlin, 1922. See p. 120

Professor Hermann. Frya reigned over all the peoples of the sea. Thus, the greatest poets and the greatest philosophers of Greece had all, without knowing it, sung of the Germanic peoples.

I have dwelt upon Zschaetzsch and Hermann because they are relatively little known. Even before Hitler took power, the man who became his foremost ideologue, A. Rosenberg, had published his famous *Myth of the Twentieth Century*. In this, the author, whose family had been among the German colonizers of the Baltic, solemnly explained that the Atlantes, the ancestors of Germanic peoples, had spread far and wide, including to Galilee, which was not to be confused with Judaea, thereby making it possible for Jesus to be Atlantan and hence a non-Jew.[27]

Within the famous Ahnenerbe Institut (the 'Institute of Ancestral Heritage'), the subject of Atlantis was frequently evoked; and it caught the interest of Reichsführer SS Heinrich Himmler himself.[28] He took a hand in spreading this Atlanto-Nationalist ideology that had been taken over from Rudbeck, throughout occupied Europe, France included.[29] As in the Age of Enlightenment, the key ploy was to change the identity of the chosen people. It was in this institute that it was first suggested that the capital of Atlantis should be identified as Heligoland (*Heiligoland*, the Holy Land).[30]

Some books *look* just like scholarly works. Their tone is measured, they have footnotes and an impeccably up-to-date bibliography; yet they are arrant ideological constructions, even lies, fabrications which, however impressive, nevertheless fail to convince. The German (Nazi) pastor Jürgen Spanuth, who practised his ministry in Bordelum, Schleswig-Holstein, wrote several such works on Atlantis.[31] The pivot upon which they hinge is the identification of Heligoland with the capital of Atlantis. These books owe much to Albert Herrmann, whose work nevertheless disappears from the bibliography of Spanuth's third book, *Die Atlanter*. Little by little, as one volume follows another, Germanic origins take up less and less space and the search for amber tends win out over the theme

19. A poster advertising the work by Sergio Frau, *Le Colonne d'Ercole. Un Inchiesta* (*The Pillars of Hercules. An Enquiry*). Rome, 2002.

of the cradle of the race. That being said, in *Die Atlanter*, Spanuth is still at pains to refute the identifications that are the most widely diffused. Atlantis is not Santorini, nor Crete, nor Tartessos, nor the Azores,[32] nor the Canaries. The royal town Basileia which, until the catastrophe of the thirteenth century BC, was sheltered by the cliffs of Heligoland, had been identified, apparently under water, in around 350 BC by Pytheas of Marseilles; and it was to visit this that the Marcellus mentioned by Proclus had sailed.[33] Himmler's heritage had gradually disappeared.

From the shores of the Baltic, let us now switch to the Mediterranean or, to be more precise, to Sardinia. When the present work was already almost completed, a book that had been launched with quite a splash came to my notice.[34] Its title translates as *The Pillars of Hercules. An Enquiry*, the subtitle being: 'How, when and why did the frontier of Heracles-Melquart, god of the West, slip definitively to Gibraltar?'[35] Its author, Sergio Frau, is a journalist; but just as there are historians who are bad journalists, there are also journalists who are good historians. Is Sergio Frau one of them?

The thesis, which is supported by, for example, Luciano Canfora, a fine scholar and a lover of paradoxes, is that the Pillars of Hercules (Fig. 19, p. 125), which, ever since Eratosthenes (third century BC), have been located at the Straits of Gibraltar, were, before the time of that geographer, situated at the Sicilian straits.[36] As for Atlantis, it is none other than Sardinia.[37] The difficulty with this thesis is that, as I have shown, what Herodotus described was the now Moroccan Atlas range of mountains; moreover, not a single ancient text supports Atlantis's identification with Sardinia. It may also be worth pointing out that Plato's Atlantis is not, as Sergio Frau repeatedly claims, an isle of 'Paradise', but instead is the domain of a Poseidon intent on harm. In these circumstances, I find myself unable to embrace this new hypothesis, however much it may gratify Sardinian patriotism.

CHAPTER 7

INTERLUDE: NOTES WITHOUT MUSIC

I have given a musical title to this brief chapter, which is to some extent an addition to the German, or rather Hitlerian section of Chapter 6, since it is devoted to two works in German that are inspired by the myth that Plato created. The first is an opera composed by Viktor Ullmann in the virtual ghetto of Theresienstadt (Terezin), in what is now the Czech Republic, with a libretto by Peter Kien. The opera was completed in 1944. It is called *Der Kaiser von Atlantis* (The Emperor of Atlantis).[1] Both the librettist and the composer disappeared in Auschwitz in October 1944.

I am not competent to comment on the music except to note that Viktor Ullmann (1898–1944) was born in Teschen (Tešin), then an Austro-Hungarian town, which later became a disputed territory claimed by both Poland and Czechoslovakia and is now divided between them. He had studied under Arnold Schönberg in Vienna. To me, the melodies of his opera are reminiscent of the airs of *The Threepenny Opera* by Brecht and Kurt Weill. The librettist, who was born in 1919, belonged to the same community.

The libretto, in four scenes, sets on stage an emperor, Overall (= Über Alles), who is introduced by the Drummer as follows: 'Attention! Attention! In the name of his Majesty the Emperor Overall! By the grace of God, our Overall, the unique glory of the country and a blessing for humanity, emperor of the two Indias, emperor of Atlantis, reigning Duke of Ophir and true esquire trenchant of

Astarte, baron of Hungary, cardinal prince of Ravenna, king of Jerusalem'. The sovereign's list of titles contains a clear allusion to the emperor who reigned in Vienna and Budapest, but his behaviour smacks more of Adolf Hitler and no doubt also of Ubu Roi.

The plot may be summarized as follows: the emperor has decreed an all-out war, but this prompts Death, in the guise of an old soldier of the Austro-Hungarian army, to go on strike. Death reminisces about the good old days of Attila and Genghis Khan but declares that his legs 'are too weak to follow motorized troops'. So now nobody can die, which also means that nobody can live. A soldier and his girl cannot love each other. For life to be possible, death must, so to speak, be resuscitated. And for this to happen, the emperor must agree to die; which he eventually does. The score is full of musical pastiches and the emperor's proclamation is sung to the tune of *Deutschland über alles*. When the dictator dies, Death assumes the appearance of the Greek god Hermes.

Apart from the title and the evocation of the totalitarian nature of this empire, allusions to Atlantis are admittedly few and far between. Of course, Plato is not named. All the same, one does sense a kind of response to those who, clustered around Himmler and a few others, identified the German Reich with Atlantis. We shall never know exactly what sources inspired the librettist. Here Atlantis symbolizes a totalitarian empire. The staging of the opera was banned in Theresienstadt, despite the fact that this community was not bereft of musical life. It was performed for the first time in Amsterdam, in 1975.[2]

The second work is a semi-autographical novel by Georges Perec (1936–82), published in 1975 by Denoël, in Paris. Its title is *W or the memory of a childhood*, and I myself was the first to spot that the story constituted a new adaptation of the myth of Atlantis.[3] Let me now recapitulate the broad lines of what I wrote at the time for a little Franco-Portuguese journal called *Sigila* (The Seal),[4] the general theme of which was secrets.

As far as I know, *W* is the only story by Georges Perec in which the author speaks of his Jewishness. As Marcel Benabou has observed, 'He may not wear his Jewishness on his sleeve as others of his generation do, but occasionally he does give it expression.'[5] Perec was born in 1936, the son of Polish Jews who had settled in France. He hardly knew his father, who volunteered for the Foreign Legion and was killed in 1940, or indeed his mother, who was deported, then murdered at the time of the great round-ups of 1942–43 in occupied Paris.

In the novel, two accounts are intertwined, in the manner of two leitmotifs in a Wagnerian opera, and they only come together at the end of the book. One text is an autobiography, the account of a childhood lived during the war and in hiding, up until the days following the liberation. At this point the orphan who, without immediately realizing it of course, was now Georges Perec, returned to Paris. This narrative is printed in a Roman font. The other narrative, printed in italics, leads us into a completely different world. The narrator is no longer Perec, but a certain Gaspard Winckler, whose date and place of birth, some time in the twentieth century, are not specified. The story describes an initiation into the mysterious world of W, an island positioned some way from the Tierra del Fuego, in the Far West. As Robert Kahn comments, 'Gaspard Winckler, the narrator of this fiction writes or says, "For a long time I searched for traces of my history ... I should like to adopt the cold, calm tone of an ethnographer: I visited this drowned world and this is what I saw there."' Perec himself writes: 'We have never found any traces of my mother or my sister. It is possible that when they were deported in the direction of Auschwitz they were taken to some other camp; it is also possible that their whole convoy was gassed upon arrival.'[6]

The 'drowned world' already seems to evoke Atlantis, but proof positive is provided by the competitive sports that take place in W. W is an island that at first sight seems a paradise: 'There are little valleys flanked by groves of oaks and plane trees, dusty paths bordered by heaps of dry stones or high bramble hedges, great fields of blueberries, turnips, maize and sweet potatoes.'[7] The two streams of warm water on the island have Greek names: Chaldes and Omega. The site of Olympia is watered by two rivers, the Alpheus and the Kladeos. Omega refers us to the last letter of the alphabet and hence also to the first, Alpha.

What is remarkable is not so much that W *is* Auschwitz but that it becomes it. Who founded W? 'A man named Wilson', whose name of course begins with a W. But who is Wilson? Perec indulges in the luxury of proposing four hypotheses. Wilson was: 1.'A lighthouse-keeper whose negligence was said to be responsible for a terrible catastrophe'; or 2. He was 'the leader of a group of convicts who mutinied while being transported to Australia'—rather like the mutineers of the Bounty—or, better still, 3. He was 'a Nemo (Jules Verne's hero), disgusted by the world and dreaming of building an ideal city', or (last hypothesis) 4. Wilson was 'a "champion" (others say a "trainer") … inspired by the Olympic enterprise' but sickened by the difficulties encountered at the end of the nineteenth century by Pierre de Coubertin, who decided to found 'a new Olympia, unassailed by chauvinistic squabbles and ideological manipulations'.[8] To those four hypotheses and the explanation that Perec himself offered: 'I wish to be a son', I will venture to suggest an addition that Perec may have considered: Wilson was the name of the American president who tipped the balance of World War I in the favour of the Allies and who dreamed of a splendid Utopia: the League of Nations, of which all that remains today is the Palais des Nations in Geneva, now in the hands of the United Nations Organization. As things eventually turned out, of course, Wilson did not even manage to get his own country to join his Utopia.

Gradually, by dint of a succession of small brush-strokes, W is transformed from a place of dreams into a nightmarish scene of cruelty. The second narrator, Gaspard Winckler, learns that Caecilia Winckler, the mother of the man whose name he has borrowed, met

with a particularly atrocious death, locked in the cabin of a ship that
was wrecked: 'When the Chilean rescue party found her, her heart
had only just ceased to beat; her fingernails had deeply lacerated the
oak door.'[9] Perec himself, speaking in his own name, provides the key
to this episode: 'I remember photographs showing the ovens clawed
by the nails of the gassed.'[10]

In the more straightforward description of W, the new Olympia
turns into Auschwitz little by little. Olympic competitions certainly
take place but are then turned into spectacles of derision: a 200-
metre race is run by club-footed cripples, and other competitions,
too, are introduced 'for laughs'. Those who do not win are docked
of their food,[11] and we later learn that those judged to be cowards
may be put to death, 'stoned and thrown to the dogs'. Perec adds
further suggestive details: 'Pitched battles break out at night in
the dormitories. Athletes are drowned in the washbasins and
lavatories.'[12] In conclusion, the narrator evokes a strictly hierar-
chical world in which one has to learn 'to squat, to stand, to stand,
to squat. Very fast, faster and faster. Run in a circle, drop to the
ground, crawl, stand up, run. Remain standing to attention for hours
and hours, for days and nights.'[13] This is a clear enough evocation of
the interminable 'roll-calls' of the world of concentration camps. As
for the performances of the athletes of the new Olympia, 'the 100
metres was run in 23.4 seconds, the 200 metres in 51'.[14] The world
of W is thus identified with the camps and, in this perspective, the
camps appear as a mockery of the Berlin Olympic Games of 1936
and all those stadium gods filmed by Leni Riefenstahl.

We know from his preparatory notes that Perec took an interest
in all that could be learnt about the Olympia of Antiquity.[15] He was
an admirer of David Rousset and of Robert Antelme, the author
of *L'Espèce humaine* (1957). And he was interested in the 'spatial'
dimension of Nazi ideology. But was he really interested in Atlantis?
On the island of W, three sets of competitions periodically take
place. The Olympiads are held every year (not every four years, as

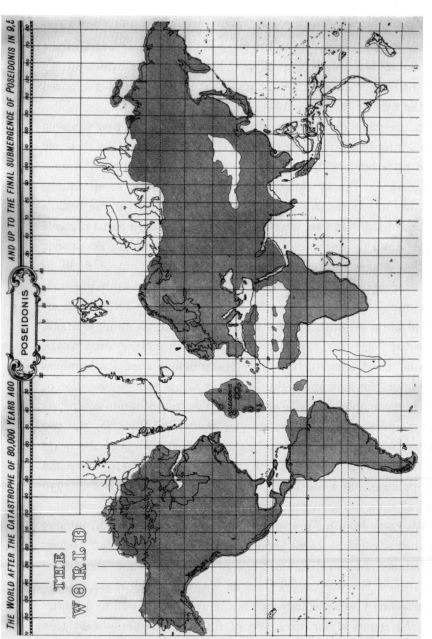

THE WORLD

THE WORLD AFTER THE CATASTROPHE OF 80,000 YEARS AGO AND UP TO THE FINAL SUBMERGENCE OF POSEIDONIS IN 9,5

POSEIDONIS

POSEIDONIS

20. The World on the eve of the submersion of Atlantis. Map taken from *The Story of Atlantis* by William Scott-Elliot, Theosophical Publishing Society, London, 1909. *See p. 137*

the real ones are). The Spartakiads which, exceptionally, are open to athletes who have not been pre-selected in their home villages, are held every three months. Might this constitute an allusion to the would-be proletarian USSR, or is it a reference to the presence of 'socialism' in Hitlerian ideology? In my opinion, the latter seems the more likely. The Atlantiads, the third set of games, take place every month. Here the allusion to Atlantis is blatant: the role that Atlantis played in Hitlerian ideology has already been noted above. Like Plato's Atlantis, the island of W is situated far to the West and is covered by luxuriant vegetation. It is a negative, regressive Utopia, what the experts call a *dystopia*, and it *turns into* Auschwitz in the same way as Atlantis turns into the world of the Other, the world of dissimilarity.

But I have still not quite finished with Perec's word-games. In a hand-written note,[16] Perec sets, alongside 'the house for the young' that is planned for W, the following strange word' '*L'Atalante*' (and this has nothing to do with Jean Vigo's well-known film entitled *Atalante*). Who was this Atalanta? She appears in yet another story handed down to us from the Greeks. She was a young huntress and an excellent runner, a wild girl raised in the mountains and suckled by a bear. She rejected marriage and was eventually defeated in a running race by the man who was to wed her, Melanion, the 'black hunter', but only as a result of the latter playing a cunning trick on her: he dropped three of Aphrodite's apples at intervals along the track, and the girl could not resist slowing down to pick them up.[17] And what form did the Atlantiades take, those monthly festivals on the island of W that were open to all the best athletes? They consisted in a rape-race. Girls who were considered to be fecund were driven on to the stadium track along which they dashed until the male athletes caught up with them and raped them. This was how children were conceived on the island of W.

And the apples? Even they are not absent from Perec's story. The mysterious figure who initiates the second narrator into the mysteries of the island of W is called Apfelstahl, 'apple of steel' or, to be more precise, 'applesteel'. All it takes to get from Atalanta to Atlantis is one dropped letter. Letter-dropping is a game to which Perec has accustomed us. In his work entitled *La Disparition* (The Disappearance), Perec contrives never to use the letter 'e'. Atlantis, too, is a tale about a disappearance, albeit admittedly not the disappearance of a letter, but that of a continent.

CHAPTER 8

WATER, EARTH AND
DREAMS

The title of this last chapter is in honour of Gaston Bachelard. I was never lucky enough to be his pupil or even to hear him lecture, but this postman-turned-professor of philosophy at the Sorbonne, who specialized in the history of science and spoke of 'restoring turbulence and aggression to reason', was a quasi-mythical figure for my generation. I would often catch a glimpse of his bearded profile, which put me irresistibly in mind of Karl Marx.

I must confess, however, that the Bachelard who fascinated me was not so much the author of *Le Nouvel esprit scientifique*, which underlined contemporary science's break away from Descartes, but rather the man who recorded his reflections on the mythology of the 'four elements' in his *Psychanalyse du feu*, *L'Eau et les rêves*, *L'Air et les songes*, *La Terre et les rêveries de la volonté*, and *La Terre et les rêveries du repos*.[1] The theory of the four elements has come down to us from ancient science and philosophy and is mentioned in Plato's *Timaeus*. It may, to some extent at least, prove a useful instrument in the ordering of some of the versions of Atlantis yet to be classified.

Earth is an element that is clearly common to them all, although the tiny island of Santorini obviously differs greatly from a continent such as America. Fire, which is present in the first version of the myth, that is to say Plato's, is not mentioned in all the others. Air is certainly present in the eventual devastating storms. I shall therefore concentrate on water, earth and dreams, as these have all figured in a whole series of texts that have played a fundamental role in the history of these imaginary representations, a history to which I offer this as my own contribution.

We have noted the appearance (one could not call it a birth) of an interaction between Atlantis and the 'occult sciences' at the end of the eighteenth century, in particular in the works of William Blake and Fabre d'Olivet. Let me now study this interaction as it appears at the end of the nineteenth century in the work of William Scott-Elliot, the spokesman of theosophy.[2] I am well aware that a theosophical Atlantis was originally created by Madame Helena Blavatsky,[3] not by Scott-Elliot. Blavatsky's string of writings, under the general title of *The Secret Doctrine*, appeared at intervals both throughout her lifetime and after her death, between 1888 and 1936 (she died in 1891). She situated the lost continent in a fictional Lemuria, positioned somewhere between Africa and South-East Asia, in such a fantastical manner that she was eventually disowned by London's Society for Psychical Research. However, I confess that I could not summon up the courage to tackle such speculations, especially since, thanks to my late, lamented friend, Simon Pembroke, I could lay my hand on a copy of the 1909 edition of *The Story of Atlantis* by Colonel William Scott-Elliot.

I own that I am not very familiar with the history of the 'occult sciences', but I fancy that their reappearance in the late nineteenth century, at the height of this positivist period, may be explained psychologically as a reaction *against* positivism. A.P. Sinnett, who prefaces Scott-Elliot's book, writes, for instance (p. ix), 'There is no limit really to the resources of astral clairvoyance in investigations concerning the past history of the earth, [when] we are concerned with the events that have befallen the human race in prehistoric epochs.' He goes on to declare that that clairvoyance allows us to enter into contact both with a past of the Earth that preceded the appearance of mankind and with 'more recent events or current accounts of episodes that have been distorted by irresponsible or perverse historians'.

One feature of this book is the inclusion of four maps representing Planet Earth in hues of pink and green. Of these four maps designed to show Earth's evolution from 1,000,000 to 9654 BC, there is one, the last, that represents the world at the Egyptian Solonian date of the submergence of the lost continent (see Fig. 20, p. 132).

It would not be particularly useful to try to summarize this millenarian history. What interested me most about it was our occultist's treatment of Plato. As early as page 3, he names Plato as the man who gave Atlantis the name Poseidonis (an assertion that is, in fact, totally false). On page 9 we are told that, according to another fantasist, Augustus Le Plongeon, one third of the vocabulary of the Mayas is Greek. The description of the capital of Atlantis is partly based on Plato (pp. 61–2), but it was certainly not from Plato that Scott-Elliot learnt that the Atlantes possessed flying machines that could be used in warfare. Plato is also used to vouch for the equality between men and women and the consumption of the blood of animals, despite the fact that in Plato the latter is a practice observed solely by the kings of Atlantis (pp. 68–9). Scott-Elliot refers far more often to the Toltec empire in what is now Mexico than to Plato. He concludes his little book with a paean of praise for the Aryan race, which is led and guided by Masters of Wisdom (pp. 86–7). The book is, still today, frequently cited and sometimes used.[4]

It is not cited but is used, structurally, by the contemporary occultists Colin Wilson and Rand Flem-Ath, who have the meridians of Planet Earth mystically starting from the Sphinx of Giza. It must be said that these authors also show great interest in the alleged 'Treasure of the Templars', which has no doubt inspired fewer 'researchers' than Atlantis, but nevertheless quite a few. On the cover of their book, these two authors felt no qualms about displaying a photograph of Albert Einstein who, admittedly, was himself sometimes a bit of a fantasist.[5]

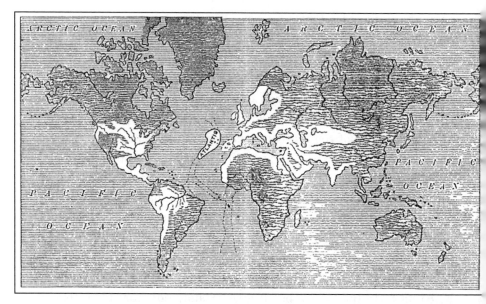

21. Atlantis and its empire, a map from *Atlantis: the Antediluvian World*, by
Ignatius Loyola Donnelly, Harper, New York, 1882.

Of all the writers who have held forth on Atlantis, none made
as great an impact or achieved such prolonged success as Ignatius
Loyola Donnelly.[6] Donnelly was born in Philadelphia into a family
of Irish extraction and he became the founder of a new town
in Minnesota in which, as time passed, he was left as the sole
inhabitant. As a supporter of the anti-slavery movement, he joined
Abraham Lincoln's Republican Party and was a deputy for Minnesota
to the Washington Congress. When defeated at the polls in 1870,
he settled down to devote himself to writing. To give some idea of
his ultra-fantastical disposition, suffice it to say that, after visiting
France in the guise of a Louis-Philippe-type bourgeois, following
the immense success of his book on Atlantis he went on to publish
further works to 'prove' that Francis Bacon was the author of the
poems of Shakespeare and Marlowe and even of Montaigne's *Essays*.
He died in 1901.

It is hard to know how to describe the thought—but perhaps that word is insufficiently subtle, so let us say the 'themes' that run through Donnelly's book. The first term (one unknown to him) that comes to mind is 'syncretism'. He gathered together and intermingled everything, all under the same hat. *Genesis*, the Bible's 'Book of the Beginning', tells of a Flood. Plato also speaks of a Flood that submerged Atlantis and swept Attica bare. In the eyes of Donnelly, these events constituted a single phenomenon. It had affected America as well as the Near East, and it made many transferences possible. What are the Greek gods? None other than the kings of Atlantis; likewise the gods of the Phoenicians. 'Semites' and 'Aryans' are all, unwittingly, Atlantes.

The second term that characterizes Donnelly—and one that he uses constantly, is 'civilization'. For him, civilization and barbarism are separated by an impassable divide. How else to explain the sudden flowering of Egypt, a phenomenon that preoccupied many minds throughout most of the nineteenth century? Under pressure from the Church, Champollion had been obliged to explain that the most ancient Egypt had not existed before 2200 BC.[7] Donnelly 'resolves' the problem by declaring that Egypt had been a colony of Atlantis, a suggestion that went far beyond anything Plato had said. And the same went for Ireland, the Iberian peninsula, the Mississipi Basin and, finally, the 'Aryans' who were destined to be the masters of the world.

In a sense, Donnelly returned to the line of questioning adopted by the thinkers of the eighteenth century, in particular Bailly, who raised the question of the origin of civilization. But whereas the reflections of the men of the Enlightenment took China, India and Egypt as their starting point, Donnelly, a contemporary of great colonial conquests, reasoned as though there had been but one Atlantic civilization and this had included the Incas of Peru as well as the Britons of the British Isles who sailed to Gaul and created France's Brittany. So convinced was Donnelly of the reality of Atlantis that he believed it would be rediscovered hundreds of fathoms beneath the Ocean. He wound up his book suggesting that, just as a century previously nobody had ever heard of Pompeii and Herculaneum (quite untrue, actually), one could imagine that the museums of the future would be rich in 'jewellery, statues, arms and tools from Atlantis'. But perhaps my simplest course is to emulate many of my predecessors and reproduce the thirteen points that Donnelly himself listed by way of a summary of his findings:[8]

1. That there once existed in the Atlantic Ocean, opposite the mouth of the Mediterranean Sea, a large island, which was the remnant of an Atlantic continent, and known to the ancient world as Atlantis.
2. That the description of this island given by Plato is not, as has long been supposed, fable, but veritable history.
3. That Atlantis was the region where man first rose from a state of barbarism to civilization.
4. That it became, in the course of ages, a populous and mighty nation from whose overflowings the shores of the Gulf of Mexico, the Mississippi River, the Amazon, the Pacific coast of South America, the Mediterranean, the west coast of Europe and Africa, the Baltic, the Black Sea, and the Caspian were populated by civilized nations.
5. That it was the true Antediluvian world; the Garden of Eden; the Garden of the Hesperides ...; the Elysian Fields ...; the Gardens of Alcinous ...; the Mesomphalos—or Navel of the Earth, a name given to the Temple at Delphi ...; the Mount Olympos ...; the Asgard—of the Eddas; the focus of the traditions of the ancient nations; representing a universal memory of a great land, where early mankind dwelt for ages in peace and happiness.
6. That the gods and goddesses of the ancient Greeks, the Phoenicians, the Hindus and the Scandinavians were simply the kings, queens and heroes of Atlantis; and the acts attributed to them in mythology, a confused recollection of real historical events.
7. That the mythologies of Egypt and Peru represented the original religion of Atlantis, which was sun-worship.

8. That the oldest colony formed by the Atlanteans was probably in Egypt, whose civilization was a reproduction of that of the Atlantic island.

9. That the implements of the 'Bronze Age' of Europe were derived from Atlantis. The Atlanteans were also the first manufacturers of iron.

10. That the Phoenician alphabet, parent of all the European alphabets, was derived from an Atlantis alphabet, which was also conveyed from Atlantis to the Mayas of Central America.

11. That Atlantis was the original seat of the Aryan or Indo-European family of nations, as well as of the Semitic peoples, and possibly also of the Turanian [Turkish] races.

12. That Atlantis perished in a terrible convulsion of nature, in which the whole island was submerged by the ocean, with nearly all its inhabitants.

13. That a few persons escaped in ships and on rafts, and carried to the nations east and west the tidings of the appalling catastrophe, which has survived to our own time in the Flood and Deluge legends of the different nations of the Old and New worlds.

Such was the colossal ambition of Ignatius Loyola Donnelly. Perhaps readers of this book will now understand why I have, in this chapter, associated his project with the dreams of William Scott-Elliot, despite the fact that in one sense the two interpretations are radically opposed. The occultist colonel belonged to the family of dreamers, whereas Donnelly's book aims to be a positivist history of Atlantis or, to be more precise, an account that will *resemble* a positivist history. Plato, similarly, sought to *resemble* Herodotus, even as he opposed him in a very radical fashion.

Donnelly was followed by successors and imitators who were far inferior to him. I will mention only one, a scholar likewise from Minnesota but who discovered Atlantis in Wisconsin's 'Devil's Lake', in the territory of an Indian people 'who dominated a large region of the American Mid-West 150 years before Christopher Columbus set sail from Spain'.[9]

Does any more need to be said? I think not. This little history of a myth that I have sketched in the wake of many others, ever since Plato launched it as one launches a projectile that will land one knows not where, is an example of what that same Plato, and Aristotle after him, in the *Poetics*, called *Mimēsis*, imitation. Ever since I began work as a historian, the practice of *Mimēsis* has fascinated me, much as art fascinated Baudelaire:

> Car c'est vraiment, Seigneur, le meilleur témoignage
> Que nous puissions donner de notre dignité
> Que cet ardent sanglot qui roule d'âge en âge
> Et vient mourir au bord de Votre éternité!

(For truly, the best proof of dignity that we can offer, O Lord, is the ardent sob that rolls down through the ages, and dies away at the edge of Your Eternity!).

Many years ago, I suggested that the best way of tackling Atlantis might be with a collection of plans of the geometric colony imagined so precisely by Plato[10] and drawn up by R. Stahel. Today I would like to recommend a book that came into my hands as I was writing the present study and that constitutes a poetic meditation on the double destiny of Venice and Atlantis.[11]

My hope is that, having stripped off the historical veneer of the myth's history, the readers of the present little book will restore the myth to the domain of images and poetry where it belongs.

Notes

Preface

1. Sub-title: *The Rewritings of a Myth.*
2. De Boccard, Paris, 1948.
3. Published in *Quaderni di storia* 16, July–December 1982, edited, in Bari, by Luciano Canfora and reprinted (with a few minor changes) in my book entitled *Les Grecs, les historiens, la démocratie, le grand écart*, La Découverte, Paris 2000. It was in 1979 that I made the acquaintance, in Pisa, of Riccardo di Donato, the Italian translator of three of my books, including this one.
4. I am delighted that this translation of my book provides an opportunity to repair that lacuna: see *Atlantide. Una controversia scientifica da Colombo a Darwin*, Carocci, Bologna, 2002. See also Marco Ciardi's article that provides information about Count Carli, 'Un Museo per la Ricerca. Gli Scienzati sabandi, il mondo antico e l'Egitto', *Mélanges Mara Miniati*, Leo Olschki, Florence, 2003, pp. 335–53.
5. I refer to this book in note 15 to my Introduction.
6. *Atlantides. Les Iles englouties*, Omnibus, Paris, 2000, 1207 pages incorporating, in particular, Jules Verne's *L'Eternel Adam*, which his son Michel published (and may have written) in 1910. The volume also contains other books written in French and in English.
7. Giovannini's article, 'Peut-on démythifier l'Atlantide?' was published in *Museum Helveticum* 42 (1985), pp. 151–6. Its key source is Pausanias VII, 24–5. See the study by René Treuil, 'L'Atlantide et l'archéologie', in *Atlantides imaginaires*, pp. 122–3.
8. I know of the programme and the publications of this colloquium thanks to the Internet surfing skills of my friend Charalampos Orfanos, whom I warmly thank for his help in this instance as well as in many others, including the composition of the present Preface.

9. I am thinking in particular of the study by Amihud Gilead, a professor at the University of Haifa, 'The Topos of Atlantis. Some philosophical insights'.

10. The authors were Filippos Tsikalas of the University of Oslo, Stavros Papamarinopoulos of the University of Patras, and V.V. Shuvalov of the Russian Academy of Sciences.

11. The first proof, announced in June 1993, contained an error. It was only just over a year later that this was rectified. I should like to thank Claudine Robert, Laurent Schwartz's daughter, for this information.

12. Thomas Kuhn, *The Structure of Scientific Revolutions*, University of Chicago Press, 1962 (1970); for a sociological critique, see Terry Shinn and Pascal Ragouet, *Controverses sur la science. Pour une sociologie transversaliste de l'activité scientifique*, Raisons d'agir, Paris, 2005, pp. 55–63.

13. Voltaire did not believe in the existence of Halley's Comet, which passes close to the earth roughly every 76 years. In his *Correspondence littéraire* of April (in reality May) 1773, Grimm unkindly wrote that Voltaire 'could not forgive even comets for momentarily distracting attention away from himself' (1810 edn, VIII, p. 196). However, Voltaire was opposed by an authentic astronomer, J.J. Le François de Lalande, who did not rule out a collision with the Earth.

14. As Marco Ciardi indicates, in *Atlantide. Una controversia scientifica da Colombo a Darwin*, p. 156, only Joseph de Guignes produced an honest and favourable review. It appeared in the *Journal des savants* of January 1781.

15. See Marco Ciardi, *Atlantide*, p. 74, citing a posthumous work dated 1841.

16. Yet again, I refer the reader to M. Ciardi, *Atlantide*, pp. 181–6.

Introduction

1. *Critias* 109b.

2. *Menexenus* 237c, trans. R.G. Bury (Loeb Classical Library). On the interpretation of the *Menexenus* and its place in the corpus of funeral orations, see—of course—Nicole Loraux's great thesis, *The Invention of Athens. The Funeral Oration in the Classical City*, trans. by Alan Sheridan, Harvard University Press, Cambridge, (Mass.) and London, 1986.

3. Belles Lettres, Paris; reprinted Macula, 1983 and 1992.

4. 'Athènes et Atlantide. Structure et statut d'un mythe platonicien'.

5. C. Gill, 'The Origin of the Atlantis Myth', *Trivium* 11 (1977), pp. 1–11; 'The Genre of the Atlantis Story', *Classical Philology* 72 (1977), pp. 287–304; 'Plato and Politics: *Critias* and the *Politicus*', *Phronesis* 24 (1979), pp. 148–62. See also his edition with commentary, *Plato: the Atlantis Story*, Bristol, 1980. Vastly inferior is the analysis of these texts by Barbara Pischel, *Die Atlantische Lehre*, Frankfurt and Berne, 1980.

6. 'The Source and Literary Form of Plato's Atlantis Narrative', in E.S. Ramage (ed.), *Atlantis. Fact or Fiction?*, Bloomington and London, 1978, pp. 49–78; see also Gianfranco Mosconi, 'L'Atlantide di Platone: spazio e tempo di un' utopia letteraria', an appendix to the book translated from Russian into Italian by I.A. Rezanov, *Atlantide tra realtà e fantasia*, Bolsena, 2002.

7. 'L'Idéologie gothisante et l' *Atlantica* d'Olof Rudbeck', *Quaderni di Storia* 11 (1980), pp. 121–56.

8. *Aux marges des dialogues de Platon. Essai d'histoire anthropologique de la philosophie ancienne*, Grenoble, 2003; this contains references to his high-quality works.

9. His first article was 'De la philosophie politique à l'épopée, le *Critias* de Platon', *Revue de Métaphysique et de Morale*, 1970, pp. 402–38. On my discussions with him, see Chapter 1 of the present work.

10. I refer several times to this colloquium, the proceedings of which have now been published: *Atlantides imaginaires*, ed. Chantal Foucrier and Lauric Guillaud, Editions Michel Houdiard, Paris, 2005. The text to which I am alluding is 'Trois lieux mythiques dans les *Dialogues* de Platon: Kallipolis, la cité des Magnètes et l'Atlantide'.

11. Academia Verlag, Sankt Augustin, Germany, 1997.

12. On this point, see the posthumous book by Cornelius Castoriadis, *Sur le Politique de Platon*, Seuil, 1999.

13. *Imagining Atlantis*, New York, Vintage Books, 1998, n. 230.

14. The 'serious' book is by Phyllis Young Forsyth, *Atlantis, the Making of Myth*, Montreal and London, 1980; the 'serious' review is the article by P.B.S. Andrews, pp. 76–9, *Greece and Rome* 14 (1967).

15. Defended in Paris IV, under the direction of Pierre Brunel. The thesis (800 pages) covers the history of the myth from the time of Plato down to 1936. An abridged version of this thesis has been published

under the title *Le Mythe littéraire de l'Atlantide (1800–1939). L'origine et la fin*, Grenoble, ELLUG, 2004.

16. Sutton Publishing, 2001. It would be unfair not to note that the first history of the myth, after Thomas-Henri Martin, whom I discuss in Chapter 1, was by Lyon Sprague de Camp, *Lost Continents: the Atlantis Theme in History*, New York, 1954, 2nd edn, 1970.

17. Here is the list, in chronological order: 'Herodote et l'Atlantide, entre les Grecs et les Juifs. Réflexions sur l'historiographie du siècle des Lumières', *Quaderni di Storia* 16 (July–December 1982), pp. 3–76, reprinted in *Les Grecs, les historiens, la démocratie*, La Découverte, 2000; 'L'Atlantide et les nations', *Représentations de l'origine. Littérature, Histoire, Civilisation*, Cahiers CRLH-CIRAOI, 4, Université de la Réunion, 1987, reprinted in *La Démocratie grecque vue d'ailleurs*, Flammarion, 1990 and 1996, pp. 139–59 (*Politics Ancient and Modern*, trans. by Janet Lloyd, Polity Press, Cambridge, 1995); 'De l'Atlantide à Masada. Réflexions sur querelle, mythe, histoire et politique', *Sigila* 10 (Autumn–Winter 2002), pp. 61–83; 'Les Atlantides', preface to the proceedings of the Cérisy colloquium (20–30 July 2002), *Atlantides imaginaires*.

18. 'L'Atlantide devant le détroit de Gibraltar? Mythe et géologie', *Comptes rendus de l'Académie des Sciences de Paris, Sciences de la terre et des Planètes* 333 (2001), pp. 233–40 (a thesis also presented in the proceedings of the Cérisy colloquium).

19. *The Flood from Heaven. Deciphering the Atlantis Legend*, New York and London, 1992. Zangger twice refers to my 1964 article.

20. Ibid., p. 227.

21. At III 89, Thucydides mentions a tidal wave that partially destroyed the island of Atlantis, in the land of the Locrian Opontes where, at the start of the Peloponnesian War, a fort stood. Possibly the name stuck in Plato's mind.

22. Cited by Richard Ellis, *Imagining Atlantis*, p. 93. He also cites a remark made by L. Sprague de Camp: 'To change all the details of the story told by Plato and claim still to be in his account is like proclaiming the legendary king Arthur 'really' to be Queen Cleopatra', *Lost Continents*, p. 80. The book by Peter D. James that is cited is *Centuries of Darkness*, 1921 (I have not seen this book).

23. 'The *Critias* and Minoan Crete', *Journal of Hellenic Studies* 33 (1913), pp. 189–206.

24. R.I. Scranton, 'Lost Atlantis found again?', *Archaeology* 2 (1949), pp. 159–62.

25. In his admirable book, *Imagining Atlantis*, Richard Ellis devotes one chapter to Minoan Crete and two others to the eruption of the Santorini volcano, respectively pp. 102–42 and 143–87. For many authors, the two hypotheses constitute a single one. Among the accounts—of a romantic nature—that are best known, James Mavor, *Voyage to Atlantis*, London and Glasgow, 1969; Jacques-Y Cousteau and Y. Piccalet, *A la recherche de l'Atlantide*, Paris, 1981; Rodney Castleden, *Atlantis destroyed*, London and New York, 1998; Igor A. Rezanov, *Atlantide tra realtà*, and Gianfranco Mosconi, L'Atlantide di Platone' see above, note 6. By and large, I myself feel close to R. Ellis and G. Mosconi.

26. See M.I. Finley's destructive criticisms of Mavor's book in the *New York Review of Books* 12 (10), 1969, pp. 38–40.

27. *Some Words about the Legend of Atlantis*, Museum of Athens, 1969.

28. R. Ellis, *Imagining Atlantis*, p. 83. The expression is borrowed from the Greek archaeologist A. Galanopoulos.

Chapter 1

1. See pages 257–333.

2. *Timaeus* 20a; the English translations of the *Timaeus* and the *Critias* are those of the Loeb Classical Library, occasionally slightly adapted.

3. See Alessandra Lukinovich, 'Un fragment platonicien: le *Critias*', *Mélanges M. Nasta*, Cluj, 2001, pp. 72–9. She concludes as follows: 'The philosophical discourse, endlessly restarted and continued, thus continually confronts the fact that it is unfinished: it is thus inevitably fragmentary.'

4. *Republic* X, 614b; the English translation is that of the Loeb Classical Library.

5. For a detailed analysis, see L. Brisson, *Platon, les mots et les mythes*, 2nd edn, La Découverte, 1995; following the first edition, (Maspero, 1982), Marcel Detienne offered a critical response to this book that is not without interest but in which the name of Herodotus is never mentioned: 'La double nature de la mythologie. Entre le *Timée* et le *Critias*', in Claude Calame (ed.), *Métamorphoses du mythe en Grèce antique*, Labor et Fides, Geneva, 1988, pp. 17–33.

6. On Plato's Egypt, see L. Brisson in *Lectures de Platon*, Vrin, 2000, pp. 151–67 and, more specifically on Atlantis, the at times overly historicist study by J. Gwyn Griffiths, 'Atlantis and Egypt', *Historia* 34 (1985), p. 3.

7. In my comparison here between Athens and Atlantis, I have used, apart from my own works and those of Luc Brisson, J.-F. Pradeau and Christopher Gill, cited in the Preface, and three articles: G. Naddaf, 'The Atlantis Myth. An introduction to Plato's later philosophy of history', *Phoenix* XLVIII (3), Autumn 1994, pp. 189–209; M.-L. Desclos, 'L'Atlantide: une île comme un corps. Histoire d'une transgression', in F. Létoublon (ed.), *Impressions d'îles*, Toulouse, P.U. du Mirail, 1996, pp. 141–55; D. Clay, 'Plato's Atlantis: the Anatomy of a Fiction', *Proceedings of the Boston Area Collegium in Ancient Philosophy*, XV (1999), pp. 1–21. Unfortunately, the little book by H.G. Nesselrath, *Platon und die Erfindung von Atlantis*, K.G. Saur, Munich and Leipzig, 2002, makes no significant contributions, being content to launch itself against doors that already stand wide open.

8. See the study by Anissa Castel-Bouchouchi, in *Atlantides imaginaires*, Proceedings of the Cérisy colloquium, July 2002.

9. See Luc Brisson, *Le Même et l'Autre dans la structure ontologique du Timée de Platon*, Klincksieck, 1974, who, for his part, is very hesitant about applying such categories to the narrative myths of both the *Timaeus* and the *Critias*.

10. See R. Brumbaugh, *Plato's Mathematical Imagination*, Bloomington U.P., Indiana, pp. 47–53. One may disagree with the symbolic interpretation of this or that figure, but it is impossible to deny the remarkable abundance of numbers.

11. See the remarks of A. Rivaud, in the CUF edition of the *Timaeus* and the *Critias*, p. 236.

12. See the useful synthesis by Marie-Dominique Richard, *L'Enseignement oral de Platon*, Preface by P. Hadot, Cerf, 1986, in particular pp. 225–33. It notes the conclusions reached by scholars such as Léon Robin in France and Konrad Gaiser and H.J. Krämer in Tübingen.

13. Rivaud, see above, n. 11, p. 237. On the names of the kings of Atlantis, see the note by Luc Brisson on p. 386 of his translation. On the subject of women, the *Critias* mentions the presence, on the acropolis of Atlantis, of statues of one hundred Nereids, aquatic deities, and of the ten kings' wives, also sculpted in gold.

14. *Platon et le miroir du mythe: de l'âge d'or à l'Atlantide*[2], PUF, 2002, pp. 252–3.

15. For a technical analysis of the description of the ports, which is obviously inspired by the Piraeus and other military ports, see F. Salviat, 'Les ports de l'Atlantide dans le *Critias* de Platon', *Mélanges Bernard Liou*, ed. Monique Mergoil, Montagnac, 2002.

16. The English translation of Lucian is that of the Loeb Classical Library, Vol. I, Book I, 2, by A.M. Harmon, 1979.

17. My remarks here are aimed at G. Naddaf who, in the article cited above (note 7), criticizes me for stressing the playful aspect of Plato's story.

18. *The Atlantis Story*, pp. xx–xxi.

19. *Le Monde de la politique*, pp. 154–79.

20. *Eos ou Platon et l'Orient*, Brussels, 1945.

21. These pages probably inspired the famous eighteenth-century poem by Lefranc de Pompignan:

> Le Nil a vu sur ses rivages
> De noirs habitants du désert
> Insulter par leurs cris sauvages
> L'astre éclatant de l'Univers.
> Cris impuissants, fureurs bizarres,
> Tandis que ces monstres barbares
> Poussaient d'insolents clameurs,
> Le Dieu continuant sa carrière
> Versait des torrents de lumière
> Sur ses obscurs blasphémateurs.

(The Nile has witnessed on its banks/ Dark-skinned desert dwellers/ Insulting with their savage cries/ The Universe's dazzling star:/ Impotent cries, strange fits of fury./ And while these barbarous monsters/ Emitted their insolent din/ God, continuing on his way,/ Showered torrents of bright light/ Upon those obscure blasphemers.) I hope I may be excused this long citation: it seemed appropriate at the time of the scorching dog-days of the summer of 2003.

22. Those are the words of J. Rufus Fears, in the book edited by E.S. Ramage, *Atlantis: Fact or Fiction?*, pp. 106–8. The very title of the book is scandalous.

23. This question was raised in Nicole Loraux's now famous article,

'Thucydide n'est pas un collègue', *Quaderni di storia* 12 (July–December 1980), pp. 53–80.

24. *Laws* III, 699ac.

25. VIII, 556c–e.

26. A. Diès, *Le Nombre de Platon. Essai d'exégèse et d'histoire*, Imprimerie national, 1936.

27. In an analysis reprinted in *The Black Hunter*, trans. by Andrew Szedey-Maszak, Johns Hopkins University Press, Baltimore, 1986, 'Plato's myth of the Statesman, the Ambiguities of the Golden Age and History', pp. 263–84. This text was the subject of a lively discussion with Luc Brisson in the course of my seminar and the ideas that he was then producing. His most recent analysis, *Lectures platoniciennes*, pp. 164–205, which was accompanied by a new translation, convinced me that I was in the wrong. In my defence, it must be said that Plato turns out to be even more perverse than I had suspected. Cornelius Castoriadis's commentary, *Sur Le Politique de Platon*, Seuil, 1999, does not challenge the traditional interpretation of the myth.

28. The Loeb Classical Library translation.

29. See, in *The Black Hunter*, my study entitled 'An Enigma at Delphi', pp. 302–24.

30. Jacques Brunschwig has written an illuminating article on this subject: 'Revisiting Plato's Cave', in J.J. Cleary and G.M. Gurtler, *Proceedings of the Boston Area Colloquium in Ancient Philosophy*, XIX (2003), Leiden and Boston, 2004, pp. 145–77.

Chapter 2

1. *Le Livre des Atlantides*, by J. Imbelloni and A. Vivante, trans. from Spanish into French by F. Gidon, Payot, 1942, pp. 14–176 provides a comprehensive list which, however, needs to be carefully checked; see also, L. Sprague de Camp, *Lost Continents: the Atlantis Theme in History and Literature*, 2nd edn, Dover, New York, 1970.

2. Athenaeus, XI, 508c–d, fr. 115, no. 259, in the Jacoby Corpus (*Fr. Gr. Hist.*); on Theopompus, see W. Robert Connor, *Theopompus and Fifth-Century Athens*, Washington, DC, Center for Hellenic Studies, Cambridge (Mass.), Harvard U.P., 1968; see also L. Canfora, in L. Firpo (ed.), *Storia delle idee politiche, economiche e sociali*, I, Turin, UTET, 1982, pp. 399–405 (bibliography, pp. 418–19).

3. Aelian's text (*On the Characteristics of Animals*, XV, 2) is translated by A.F. Schofield, in the Loeb Classical Library, 1958; in Jacoby *Fr. Gr. Hist.* it is no. 115, f. 75. Jacoby also cites Servius, *Commentary on Virgil*, Bucolics VI, 13, 26.

4. *De Caelo*, II, 14, 298a.

5. This text from the *Meteorologica* is cited by Proclus in his *Commentary on the Timaeus*, 188, 22.

6. See P. Moraux, *Les Listes anciennes des ouvrages d'Aristote*, Louvain, 1951, pp. 161–3; the reference to this passage in the Bekker edition is 836b30–837a. Remarkably enough, an altogether analogous text is to be found in Diodorus Siculus, V, 19.

7. *Essays* I, XXXI, translated by M.A. Screech, Penguin Books, London, 1991, pp. 229–31.

8. I refer the reader to my essay, 'Diodore et le vieillard de Crète', which prefaced Michel Casevitz's French translation of Books I and II of the *Bibliothèque historique*, coll. 'La Roue à Livres', Belles Lettres, 1991. It has also been reprinted in my *Les Grecs, les historiens, la démocratie*, pp. 135–55.

9. See the edition of Diodorus, Book III, CUF by Bibiane Bommelaer, note 2, p. 2.

10. See B. Bommelaer, ibid., III, xi and xli–xliv.

11. The *Olympieum* was completed under Hadrian, after Plutarch's death. It was begun under Pisistratus.

12. This analysis stems from an account of an earthquake in Nicomedia (24 August, AD 358).

13. *De Aeternitate Mundi*, 19.

14. He was killed when Vesuvius erupted in AD 79.

15. J. Pouilloux, in his French translation of *De Aeternitate Mundi* (ed. Arnaldez, 1969) translates *ou plōton* as 'Elle n'est pas seulement navigable' (It is not only navigable), which I consider to be impossible. The whole passage from 117 on is attributed to Theophrastus by H. Diels, *Doxographi Graeci, The Opinions of Physicians*, fr. 12, Berlin, 1879. The same attribution is made by W.W. Fortenbaugh et al., *Theophrastus of Eresus, Sources for his Life, Writings, Thoughts and Influence*, I, Leiden, New York and Cologne, Brill, 1992, p. 351; the reference in Philo's treatise is 139–41. To get the text to refer to mud, it has to be emended, as has sometimes been suggested.

16. Fr. 10, p. 130 Leemans = 8 p. 51 Des Places (cited by Clement of

Alexandria, *Stromateis* I, 22, and subsequently also Eusebius of Caesarea, *Ecclesiastical History* IX, 7, 9 and XI, 10, 14).

17. Tertullian, *Apology*, XL, 2-4. It is worth noting that Tertullian had read Diodorus Siculus (ibid. X, 7) and knew that Saturn (Cronos) was just a man. He also alludes to the disappearance of Atlantis, as just one of the examples of change in the world, in *De Pallio* II, 3, written during the last years of his life.

18. *Contre les Gentils*, I, 5, 1, ed. H. Le Bonniec, Belles Lettres, 2nd edn, 2002.

19. To this reference, we may add the only example of an allegorical reinterpretation of the Atlantis War, namely the very brief mention by Clement of Alexandria, *Stromateis* 9, 58.

20. In the 'Histoire' Collection, Belles Lettres, 1990.

21. PUF, 2nd edn, 1972, p. 162: 'He might deserve to be considered as a saint.'

22. I am citing vol. I of the *Commentaire sur le Timée*, Vrin, 1966. I have very few reservations with regard to this translation, but one is that I would speak of the Atlantes rather than the Atlantins. (Translator's note: I have based this translation of Proclus's commentary on Festugière's translation combined with that by Thomas Taylor, published by The Prometheus Trust, 1998, Frome, Somerset.)

23. *A Commentary on the Timaeus*, Oxford U.P., 1928.

24. Proclus, *Commentary*, 4, 25, Festugière, p. 27.

25. In the French translation, Festugière points out that 'réellement' (really) is his own (justifiable) addition.

26. Festugière did not notice the allusion to Aristotle and thinks, p. 246, note 2, that 'Proclus must be reproducing a current objection'.

27. See Festugière's note 2 on p. 233. This Marcellus, who reappears at 182-15 as the author on an *Enquiry on Ethiopia*, is otherwise unknown. Festugière thinks there must be some confusion with a certain Marcianus, but the latter wrote 'A Journey round the Outer Sea' that does not appear to relate to Ethiopia at all. In the Jacoby Corpus, the fragments cited by Proclus are indicated by the number 671.

28. I am here summarizing the translation of the Greek text 76, 20-80 8. Amelius travelled in Italy and served as Plotinus's secretary for 21 years, producing a chronological edition of his works; see the remarks of Luc Brisson in Richard Goulet (ed.), *Dictionnaire des philosophes*

antiques, I, CNRS, 1989, pp. 160-4. Scholars disagree as to whether there were two Origens (one Christian, the other neo-Platonist) or only one. See, for example, Henri Crouzel, *Origène, Le Sycomore*, Paris and Namur, 1985, pp. 29-31.

29. On Cosmas, see W. Wolska, *La Topographie chrétienne de Cosmas Indicopleustès*, 'Bibliothèque byzantine', Etudes, 1962. The same person, now named Wanda Wolska-Conus, produced a new and remarkable edition of the text in the 'Sources chrétiennes' collection published by Cerf (3 volumes, 1968-73). This admirable edition reproduces the illustrations contained in three manuscripts.

30. *Hellēnes*: I believe that this should be understood to mean 'pagans'.

31. Wanda Wolska-Conus, the editor, notes that the same distorted citation from the *Timaeus* 22b reappears two and a half centuries later in Eusebius, Chronicle I, cols 3-4, and also in the same Eusebius, *Ecclesiastical History* X, 4, 19. The Christians thus seem to have found a way to appropriate the exclamation addressed to Solon: 'Solon, Solon, you Greeks are eternal children!'.

Chapter 3

1. See Aldo Schiavone's admirable work, *L'Histoire brisée. La Rome antique et l'Occident moderne*, trans. into French by Jean and Geneviève Bouffartigue, Paris, Belin, 2003.

2. See the edition produced within the framework of Plato in Latin by Raymond Klibansky and J. Waszink, *Timaeus a Calcidio translatus commentarioque instructus*, London and Leiden, Brill, 1962. The commentary shows that the Hebrew influence on Plato is considered to be self-evident, but shows no interest at all in Atlantis.

3. See the preface by Brian Merrilees, *The Anglo-Norman Voyage of Saint Brendan*, Manchester University Press, Manchester, 1979.

4. See R. Marcel, *Marsile Ficin, 1433-1499*, Belles Lettres, 1958, pp. 630-1, and, for the context, J.-C. Saladin, *La Bataille du grec à la Renaissance*, Belles Lettres, 2000.

5. Although Alexandre de Humboldt, in his *Examen critique de l'histoire de la géographie du Nouveau Continent*, 5 vols, Paris, 1836-39, notes (I, p. 167) the absence of Atlantis from all Columbus's writings, he nevertheless declares that Columbus 'liked to remember Solon's Atlantis' (I, p. 30). The admiral's son, engaged in a polemic against

Oviedo, was later to state formally that his father showed no interest in Plato's story; see *The Life of the Admiral Christopher Columbus by his son Ferdinand*, trans. and annotated by B. Keen, Rutgers U.P., 1959, pp. 28–34. For the reference to Piero Martirio d'Anghiera, see G. Randles, 'Le Nouveau Monde, l'Autre Monde et la pluralité des mondes', *Congreso internacional de Historia dos Descobrimentos*, Lisbon, 1961, IV, pp. 347–82.

6. *Tristes Tropiques*, Plon, coll. Terre Humaine, 1984, p. 79 (*World on the Wane*, translated by John Russell, Hutchinson, London, 1961, p. 78).

7. I have found two books useful: Ida Rodriguez Prampolini, *L'Atlantida de Platon en las Cronistas del siglo XVI*, Junta Mexicana de investigationes historicas, Mexico, 1947, and, above all, G. Gliozzi, *Adamo e il nuovo mondo: la nascita dell'antropologia come ideologia coloniale (1500–1700)*, La Nuova Italia, Florence, 1976, pp. 178–246. This essential book stresses in particular the part played in this debate by pro- and anti-Spanish polemics.

8. *Historias de las Indias* (1527); I consulted the edition by J. Perez de Tudela Bueso, Madrid, Biblioteca de autores españoles, 1957, pp. 36–9.

9. Thanks to Riccardo Di Donato's friendly help, I have been able to consult the edition published with an Italian translation by Sebastiano Degli Antoni, Bologna, 1738; Chantal Foucrier brought two French translations to my attention, one by Philippe Macquer and Jacques Lacombe (Paris, Quillau, 1753) and one in verse, with a commentary by Prosper Yvaren, Paris, 1847.

10. On these questions, the basic work is A. Borst, *Der Turmbau von Babel. Geschichte der Meinungen über Ursprung und Vielfalt der Sprachen und Völker*, 6 vols, Stuttgart, A. Hierseman, 1957–63. More particularly, on Noah, see D.C. Allend, *The Legend of Noah, Renaissance Rationalism in Art, Science and Letters*, Urbana, University of Illinois Press, 1949, and B. Branell, 'The Sons of Noah and the Construction of Ethnic and Geographical Identities in the Medieval and Early Modern periods', *The Willliam and Mary Quarterly* LIV (1), January 1993, pp. 93–142; see also L. Poliakov, *Le mythe aryen. Essai sur les sources du racisme et du nationalisme*, Calmann-Lévy, Paris, 1971, 2nd edn, Editions Complexe, Brussels, 1987, and M. Olender, *Les Langues du Paradis*, Seuil, 1989.

11. See T. Parfitt, *The Lost Tribes of Israel. The History of a Myth*, Weidenfeld & Nicholson, London, 2002, pp. 25–35; see also A. Destremaux and

F. Schmidt, *Moïse géographe. Recherches sur les représentations juives et chrétiennes de l'espace*, Vrin, 1988, (ignored by T. Parfitt). For a history of the genealogical tree, see Christiane Klapisch-Zuber, *L'Ombre des ancêtres. Essai sur l'imaginaire médiéval de la parenté*, Fayard, Paris, 2000.

12. See T. Parfitt, n. 11 above, p. 2.

13. See vol. III, p. 105.

14. Gliozzi, *Adamo e il nuovo mondo*, p. 184. See Chapter 3, n. 7.

15. See A. Gerbi, *La Natura delle Indie nuove da Cristoforo Colombo a Gonzalo Fernandez de Oviedo*, Riccardo Ricciardi, Naples, 1975. For the letter from Charles V, see pp. 379–80. This whole argument stems from a famous forger, Annius of Viterbo who, although based in Italy, received a pension from the king of Spain.

16. J. Goropius Becanus, 'Hispanica' in *Opera*, Antwerp, 1580 (the author died in 1574), p. 35, 62, 105–8; see Gliozzi, above, n. 14, pp. 42–4, 155–8. Becanus's hispanophilia did not prevent him from detecting a kinship between the Indian languages and Flemish; for a retrospective history of Spanish speculations on the identity of America, see G. Garcia, *Origen de los Indios del Nuevo Mundo*, Valencia, 1603; on Atlantis, see pp. 351–406. Lastly, we should remember that in Camoens's *The Lusiads*, Odysseus is the founder of Lisbon.

17. See the edition produced by P. Carmelo Saenz de Santa Maria, Madrid, Atlas, 1960, pp. 201–5.

18. See Book I, chapter XX; I have cited the French title because Gomara has been translated into French (Payot, 1979), but that translation is so poor that it is preferable to consult either the original Spanish or the 1595 French translation; see the fundamental article by M. Bataillon, 'L'Unité du genre humain du P. Acosta au P. Clavigero', *Mélanges Jean Sarrailh*, I, Centre de Recherches de l'Institut d'études hispaniques, 1966, pp. 75–95.

19. The English translation is by M.A. Screech, Penguin Books, London, 1991. The examples show that Montaigne was familiar with what Pliny the Elder, cited above, had said.

20. Gliozzi, *Adamo e il nuovo mondo*, pp. 199–219; see also, on Montaigne's sources, M. Bataillon, 'Montaigne et les Conquérants de l'or', *Studi Francesi* 9 (1959), pp. 352–67.

21. See Gliozzi, *Adamo e il nuovo mondo*, pp. 220–30.

22. I am citing the translation and lavish commentary by Michèle Le

Doeuff and Margaret Llasera, *La Nouvelle Atlantide, suivie du Voyage dans la pensée baroque*, Payot, 1983, reprinted coll. GF, 1993. For a comparison between Bacon, Thomas More, *Utopia* (1516) and Tommaso Campanella, *Civitas Solis, Idea Reipublicae Platonica*, Frankfurt, 1623, see F.R. White (ed.), *Famous Utopias of the Renaissance*, Hendricks House, New York, 1955. It is worth noting that Campanella was an admirer of Galileo. Finally, a commentary by Chantal Foucrier is to be found in *L'Autre et le Même. Pratiques de réécritures*, edited by herself and D. Mortier, Publications de l'Université de Rouen, 2001, pp. 133–46. I also consulted the studies by M. de Gandillac and Marie-Agnès Manry, presented at the Cérisy Colloquium (20–30 July 2002): *Atlantides imaginaires. Réécritures d'un mythe*, C. Foucrier and L. Guillaud (ed.), Michel Houdiard, Paris, 2005 (with a preface by myself). Bacon was to acquire a late disciple in the person of Condorcet, who produced a fragment entitled 'Atlantide ou efforts combinés de l'espèce humain pour le progrès des sciences'. It is to be found in the magnificent *Tableau historique des progrès de l'ésprit humain*, edited by J.P. Schandeler and P. Crépel, INED, 2004, pp. 873–949. I should like to thank Yvon Garlan, a contributor to this work, for presenting me with a copy of it.

23. *City of God* XII, 10 and XVIII, 40.

24. *Praeadamitae, sive exercitatis quibus traducuntur Primi Homines ante Adamum conditi*. The book was translated into English as early as 1656. I know of two excellent works on La Peyrère: Jean-Pierre Oddos, *Recherches sur la vie et l'oeuvre d'Isaac La Peyrère, thèse de 3e cycle*, Grenoble, 1977, and Richard H. Popkin, *Isaac La Peyrère (1596–1676), His life, Work and Influence*, Leiden, Brill, 1987.

25. *Praeadamitae*, pp. 176–80 in the original edition.

26. Martin, 'Dissertation on Atlantis', in *Studies on Plato's Timaeus*, pp. 272–3.

27. There exists a modern Swedish edition in five volumes, edited by Axel Nelson, Uppsala, 1937–1950. Vol. IV, pp. 205–65 contains a valuable collection of records relating to the work's reception. I myself studied the Latin text of the original edition. The bibliography is truly colossal. Let me cite in particular J. Svenning, *Zur Geschichte des Goticismus*, Uppsala and Stockholm, Almqvist och Wieksell, 1967; J. Svenbro (my adviser on this subject), 'L'Idéologie gothicisante et *L'Atlantica* d'Olof Rudbeck', *Quaderni di Storia* 11 (January–June

1980), pp. 121–56; G. Eriksson, *The Atlantic Vision. Olaus Rudbeck and Baroque Science*, Science History Publications, Uppsala Studies in History of Science, 1994; also by G. Eriksson, *Rudbeck, 1630–1702, Lis, Lärdom, Dröni Baroqckens Sverige, Atlantis*, Stockholm, 2002. On polemics on Gothicism in Germany and Scandinavia, Dieter Lohmeier, 'Das gotische Evangelium und die Cimbrischen Heiden', *Lychnos*, 1977–78, pp. 54–70.

28. See A. Ellenius, 'Olaus Rudbecks Atlantiska Anatomi', *Lychnos*, 1959, pp. 40–52, with a summary in English, pp. 53–4.

29. See G. Eriksson, n. 27 above, p. 160.

30. *Atlantica* I, p. 890.

31. On whom the major work is Elisabeth Labrousse, *Pierre Bayle*, Albin Michel, 1996; she points out, p. 194, n. 32, that the dictionary contains no entry on *Plato*.

32. A. Audigier, *L'Origine des Français et de leur Empire*, Paris, 1676.

33. Ibid., pp. 214–17; for a brief study, see J.R. Stager, 'France: the Holy Land, the Chosen People and the Most Christian King', *Mélanges C.H. Harbison*, F.K. Rabb and J.E. Seigel (ed.), Princeton U.P., 1969.

34. See G. Costa, *Le Antichità germaniche nella cultura italiana da Machiavelli a Vico*, Naples, Bibliopolis, 1977, pp. 372–3.

35. The publication of *Mundus Subterraneus* in Amsterdam suggests that this Jesuit was not entirely orthodox; see J. Godwin, *Athanasius Kircher, a Renaissance Man and the Quest for Lost Knowledge*, London, 1979. I am grateful to Marcel Gauchet for this reference; the recent collection edited by Paula Findlen, *Athanasius Kircher, the Last Man who Knew Everything*, New York and London, 2004, does not mention his cartography of Atlantis.

36. See J.B.M. Bory de Saint-Vincent, *Essai sur les îles Fortunées et l'antique Atlantide*, Paris, year XI (1803). Bory de Saint-Vincent criticizes Rudbeck severely: 'To glorify his country, did Rudbeck really need to seek within it for a country that never existed? Was it not enough for him that Sweden produced Linnaeus?', p. 445.

37. N. Stenton, *Opera philosophica* (U. Marr ed.), Copenhagen, 1910, 2, p. 224; see P. Rossi, *The Dark Abyss of Time*, Chicago, 1984, p. 19. I am obliged to Alain Schnapp for these references; see his book, *La Conquête du passé*, 2nd edn, Le Livre de Poche, Paris, 1998.

Chapter 4

1. The problem is tackled by Frank E. Manuel, *The Eighteenth Century Confronts the Gods*, Cambridge (Mass.), 1959, in particular p. 7 and 245–80, and, even more directly, by Peter Gay, *The Enlightenment. An Interpretation. The Rise of Modern Paganism*, London, 1966.

2. 'Le Mythe au XVIIIe siècle', *Critique* 366 (Nov. 1977). pp. 975–97; I am citing p. 985.

3. See A. Dupront, *Pierre-Daniel Huet et l'exégèse comparative au XVIIe siècle*, Paris, 1930.

4. C.-M. Olivier's dissertation may be found in M. de Salengre, *Continuation des Mémoires de littérature et d'histoire*, Paris, 1726, pp. 19–45; I am citing pp. 29–30.

5. *Observationes sacrae quibus varia Sacri Codicis utriusque foederis loca illustrantur*, pp. 381–415 (with reference to Olivier).

6. See J. Euvremius, *Atlantica Orientalis sive Atlantis*, Berlin, Stralsung and Leipzig, 1764, the Latin translation of a book published in Swedish in 1754; and finally F. Baer (pastor at the Swedish embassy in Paris), *Essai historique et critique sur les Atlantiques dans lequel on se propose de faire voir la conformité qu'il y a entre l'histoire de ce peuple et celle des Hébreux*, Paris, 1762, with a polemic against Euvremius, p. 10. F. Baer, in his turn, became the target of a devastating critique by Diderot, see *Correspondance inédite de Grimm et Diderot*, XV, 1829, pp. 160–72.

7. On this group, see *Les Grecs, les historiens, la démocratie*, La Découverte, Paris, 2000, pp. 59–60. Let me reassure all those who may be concerned by the matter, that Abbé Bonnaud, who died in a massacre in 1792, is completely unrelated to my friend Robert Bonnaud, the author of numerous works in the historical field. It was François Hartog who brought to my attention the completely dotty book by Abbé Bonnaud, from which I cite pp. 172–3. Bonnaud's book was reprinted after the Restoration by Gauthier, Besançon and Paris, 1824. It was first reprinted in 1790.

8. *Œuvres complètes*, Garnier, Paris, 1878–85, XXX, p. 390; see also 'Lettre à M. Panckouke', dated 30 April 1777, ed. Bestermann, 128, Banbury, 1976, p. 251.

9. On this debate, the essential work is A. Gerbi, *La Disputa del Nuovo Mondo. Storia di una polemica 1750–1900*, Milan and Naples, 1955 (reprinted in 1983). Carli is heavily involved (see the index).

10. On Carli, the most complete and accurate study is that by F. Venturi, in his edition of *Riformatori Lombardi, Piemontesi e Toscani*, Milan and Naples, 1954, vol. III in the series *Illuministi Italiani*, pp. 419–38. So far as my interest is concerned, Carli's main work is his series of letters, *Lettere americane* (1770–81). The first two have been translated into French: *Lettres américaines dans lesquelles on examine l'origine, l'état civil, politique et religieux, les arts, l'industrie, les sciences, les moeurs, les usages des anciens habitants de l'Amérique, les grandes époques de la nature, l'ancienne communication des deux hémisphères et la dernière révolution qui a fait disparaître l'Atlantide ...*, written in Boston, published Paris, 1788; for the Italian edition, see the *Opere* of Count Carli, Milan, 1779f.: the third and fourth series can be found in vols XIII and XIV.

11. *Lettres américaines*, I, letter 26, II, letter 45, p. 387.

12. Ibid., II, letter 45, p. 428.

13. I have summarized *Lettres américaines*, II, p. 485.

14. *Lettres américaines*, I, p. 87; II, p. 405 and passim.

15. *Opere*, XIV, 82f.

16. Carli's theories do not appear to have made much impact outside Italy and France, where his Letters were translated. Nevertheless, I find that they were cited by the Jesuit Juan de Velasco who, shortly after, produced a study of the kingdom of Quito: see *Historia Natural del Reino de Quito*, Quito (Ecuador), I, 1970, p. 269. Velasco was, of course, only interested in the American aspects of Carli's theories. I am grateful to Geneviève Teitgen for this reference.

17. The nine volumes by Court de Gébelin that appeared under this title, in Paris, between 1773 and 1782, make no mention of Atlantis. The only Atlantes known to Gébelin were those of Diodorus; see *Monde primitif*, I, 2nd branch, 1st subject, pp. 26, 32, 34. I am grateful to F. Récanati, who kindly checked this reference for me.

18. The theme appears in *Histoire de l'Astronomie ancienne depuis son origine jusqu'à l'établissement de l'Ecole d'Alexandrie*, Paris, 1775; it reappears and is developed in *Lettres sur l'Origine des Sciences et sur celle des peuples de l'Asie adresssées à M. de Voltaire*, London and Paris, 1777, and above all in *Lettres sur l'Atlantide de Platon et sur l'ancienne histoire de l'Asie*, London and Paris, 1779.

19. Letter-preface to *Lettres sur l'Origine*, p. 4.

20. *Lettres sur l'Origine*, p. 16.

21. *Lettres sur l'Atlantide*, p. 19.
22. *Lettres sur l'Origine*, p. 156.
23. Bailly cites and refutes Baer, *Lettres sur l'Atlantide*, pp. 108–12. He also rejects the American hypothesis, ibid., pp. 86–92.
24. *Lettres sur l'Origine*, p. 103.
25. *Lettres sur l'Atlantide*, p. 59, 332.
26. Ibid., p. 108.
27. *Lettres sur l'Origine*, p. 54.
28. *Lettres sur l'Atlantide*, p. 83.
29. After publishing a relatively favourable review (*Journal des Savants*, January 1779, pp. 15–23), the periodical slated Bailly (February, pp. 93–110). For further biographical details, see *Les Grecs, les historiens, la démocratie*, p. 63, n. 139.
30. 'Gibbon's Contribution to historical method' (1954), in *Studies in Historiography*, Weidenfeld and Nicolson, Worcester and London, 1966, pp. 40–56.
31. On Fréret, see C. Grell and Catherine Volpilhac-Auger (ed.), *Nicolas Fréret, Légende et vérité, Actes du Colloque des 18 et 19 octobre 1991, Clermont-Ferrand*, Oxford, Voltaire Foundation, 1994, which contains a full bibliography. On Fréret and French history, see the information provided by C. Nicolet, *La Fabrique d'une nation. La France entre Rome et les Germains*, Perrin, 2003. On ancient historiography in the eighteenth century, see Chantal Grell, *L'Histoire entre érudition et philosophie. Etudes sur la connaissance historique à l'âge des Lumières*, PUF, 1993 and *Le XVIIIe siècle et l'antiquité en France, 1680–1789*, Oxford, Voltaire Foundation, 1995.
32. Histoires et Mémoires de l'Académie des Inscriptions ..., vol. 23, 1749–51, 'Observations sur les deux déluges ou inondations d'Ogygès et de Deucalion', pp. 129–48; I cite p. 132.
33. *Essai sur les moeurs*, in *Œuvres complètes*, XI, pp. 3–5.
34. J. D'Anville, *Géographie ancienne abrégée*, III, Paris, 1768, pp. 122–3.
35. *Mundus subterraneus*, I, p. 82; on Kircher, see above, chapter 3, n. 35.
36. See J.B.M. Bory de Saint-Vincent, *Essai sur les îles Fortunées et l'antique Atlantique*, Paris, Year XI (1803), pp. 427–522, which refers explicitly to Kircher and refutes other hypotheses, including those relating to Sweden and Palestine.
37. For a recent example, see P. Mayol in *Océans*, 78 (May 1981), pp. 6–22,

a document brought to my attention by Jean Railhac. I do not think André Breton alluded to this hypothesis in the magnificent pages that he devoted to the Canaries in *L'Amour fou*.

38. J. Pitton de Tournefort, *Relation d'un voyage au Levant*, ed. In-8°, Lyons, 1717, letter XV, II, p. 409.

39. His principal book, *L'Antiquité dévoilée par ses usages ou examen critique des principales opinions, cérémonies et institutions religieuses et politiques des différents peuples de la terre*, 3 vols, Amsterdam, 1766 [November 1765] is posthumous. On Boulanger, I have used, essentially, the works of P. Sadrin, his *thèse du 3e cycle*, in 2 vols, published by Belles Lettres (Publications de l'Université de Dijon), in 1978. The first vol. reproduces the second edition of *L'Antiquité dévoilée* (Amsterdam, 1766), his biographical and synthetic essay, *Nicolas-Antoine Boulanger (1722–1759) ou avant nous le déluge*, The Voltaire Foundation, Oxford, 1986. But see also F. Venturi, *L'Antichità svelata e l'idea del progresso in N.A. Boulanger ...*, Bari, 1947. Neither Venturi, naturally enough, nor Sadrin mentions Atlantis, although the latter did know of the unpublished manuscript in which Boulanger wrote on the subject.

40. *Recherches sur l'origine du despotisme oriental* [Geneva], 1761, section 6, pp. 60–1, cited by Sadrin, *Nicolas-Antoine Boulanger*, p. 67.

41. Ibid., 1765 edn, Paris, p. 54.

42. *Antiquité dévoilée*, II, pp. 325–404.

43. No. 869.

44. See the edition of *Epoques* by J. Roger, Paris, 1962, pp. LXXVI and LXXVII. On chronological disputes in the seventeenth and eighteenth centuries, in particular about fossils, see Paolo Rossi, *I Segni del Tempo. Storia della Terra e Storia delle Nazioni da Hooke a Vico*, Milan, 1979. The references to Boulanger are plentiful, but Atlantis is hardly mentioned; see, however, p. 36.

45. See the preface to his edition, with commentary, of *L'Antiquité*, p. 39.

46. The essential information is to be found on pages 109–16 of the Museum manuscript. On its rediscovery, see J. Roger, 'Un manuscrit perdu et retrouvé: les 'Anecdotes de la nature''. *Revue des Sciences humaines*, 1953, pp. 231–54. This manuscript was identified by J. Hampton, *Boulanger et la science de son temps*, Geneva and Lille, 1955. The date of publication is later than J. Roger's work, but the discovery was prior to it.

47. See his *Chronology of Ancient Kingdoms Amended*, London, 1728.

48. *Origines des premières sociétés, des peuples, des sciences, des arts et des idiomes anciens et modernes*, Amsterdam (to be found in Paris), 1769.

49. On Bartoli, see P.A. Paravia, *Della vita e degli studi di Giuseppe Bartoli*, Turin, 1842, a book that I was able to read thanks to G. Cambiano (Turin) and W.R. Thalmann (Yale University); on the meeting with Gibbon, see G.A. Bonnard (ed.), *Gibbon's Journey from Geneva to Rome. His Journal from 20 April to 2 October 1764*, London, Paris, Melbourne, 1961, p. 22. Forty years ago, I helped to resuscitate this figure. My remarks have been repeated and considerably developed by J.-F. Pradeau, in his book that is cited in the Introduction to the present work; see also his article 'Le Poème politique de Platon. Giuseppe Bartoli: un lecteur moderne du récit atlante', in *Le Timée de Plato. Contributions à l'histoire de sa réception*, Editions de l'Institut supérieur de philosophie, Louvain-La Neuve, 2000.

50. See the chapter devoted to Sweden by Venturi, *Settecento riformatore*, III, *La Prima Crisi dell' Antico Regime (1768–1776)*, Turin, 1979, pp. 281–342.

51. Bartoli, *Discours par lequel Sa Majesté le roi de Suède a fait l'ouverture de la Diète, en suédois, traduit en français et en vers italiens, avec un essai sur l'explication historique que Platon a donnée à son Atlantide et qu'on a pas considérée jusqu'à présent ...*, Stockholm, 1779, pp. 190–1.

52. Ibid., pp. 106–7 and 224–5.

53. *Etudes sur le Timée de Platon*, II, p. 280.

54. See the edition, organized by Guido Abbatista, of *Considérations philosophiques, historiques et géographiques sur les deux mondes 1780–1804*, Scuola Normale Superiore, Pisa, 1993, p. 312.

Chapter 5

1. See F. Hartog, *The Mirror of Herodotus*, trans. by Janet Lloyd, University of California Press, Berkeley, Los Angeles, London, 1988, pp. 301–3, and my observations in *Les Grecs, les historiens, la démocratie*, p. 59.

2. *Philosophie de la nature*, 6 vols, London, 1777, IV, pp. 245–8.

3. *Histoire des hommes*, I, pp. xiii and p. 7.

4. Ibid., I, pp. 50–1.

5. Ibid., II, p. 14.

6. Ibid., I, pp. lxviii and p. 227.

7. Ibid., II, p. 11.

8. Ibid., I, p. 227, II, pp. 16 and passim.

9. *Le Génie du Christianisme*, I, IV, 2, Paris, Year X, I, pp. 143–4. The allusion to a 'primitive world' is aimed partly at Delisle de Sales but also at Court de Gébelin, the author of the nine volumes of *Le Monde primitif*, 1773–82, in which the Atlantes of Diodorus, but not those of Plato, make a brief appearance, I, pp. 28–32, 34.

10. P. Leroux, *La Grève de Samarez*, ed. J.-P. Lacassagne, Paris, 1979, II, p. 447. On Fabre d'Olivet, the fundamental book is that by Léon Cellier, *Fabre d'Olivet. Contribution à l'étude des aspects religieux du Romantisme*, Paris, 1957; a book that is very important for a study of Delisle de Sales is that by A. Viatte, *Les Sources occultes du Romantisme. Illuminisme—Théosophie*, Albin-Michel, 1928, reprinted 1969.

11. The little book by G. Scholem, *Du Frankisme au Jacobinisme*, Seuil-Gallimard, 1981, has nothing new to add on this point.

12. See L. Cellier,, n. 10 above, pp. 12–15.

13. See the correction in no. 8, 27 May, p. 32.

14. Fabre d'Olivet's principal works are *Lettres à Sophie sur l'histoire*, 2 vols, Paris, Year XI (1805); *De l'Etat social de l'homme ou vues philosophiques du genre humain*, 2 vols, Paris, 1822; *Histoire philosophique du genre humain*, 2 vols, Paris, 1822; *Histoire philosophique du genre humain*, 2 vols, Paris, 1824.

15. *Lettres à Sophie*, I, pp. 206–84 (citation, p. 206).

16. To which the reference is ibid., p. 3.

17. Ibid., II, p. 7.

18. *Histoire du genre humain*, I, p. 5.

19. Ibid., I, pp. 67–8.

20. Ibid., pp. 135–6.

21. Ibid., pp. 190–2.

22. Ibid., p. 263 and passim.

23. Ibid., p. 234 and 256.

24. According to the respective titles of C. Froidefond, Aix and Gap, 1971, and F. Cumont, Brussels, 1937.

25. *Histoire du genre humain*, I, pp. 308–9.

26. Ibid., p. 189. Fabre is by no means consistent; he calls 'Atlantes' now *Sudéens* (Southerners), now 'the red (*Austréenne*) race that civilized them.

27. Ibid., pp. 188–9, 195–6, 309–10.

28. Ibid., p. 320.
29. Ibid., pp. 326–35.
30. Ibid., p. 81.
31. Ibid., p. 193.
32. Ibid., p. 125.
33. See, in the collection entitled *Atlantides imaginaires*, to which I wrote a preface, the study by Nicole Fernandez-Bravo.
34. On the place of Cousin and T.-H. Martin in Platonic studies, see P. Vermeren, *Victor Cousin. Le jeu de la philosophie et de l'Etat*, L'Harmattan, Paris, 1995, and, before him, E.M. Manasse, *Bücher über Platon, III, Werke in Französischer Sprache*, Tübingen, 1976; the Foreword by R. Brague to the reprint of the work by T.-H. Martin, and also H. Wismann, '*Modus interpretandi*, Analyse comparée des études platoniciennes en France et en Allemagne au XIXe siècle', in M. Bollack and H. Wismann, *Philologie und Hermeneutik im 19. Jahrhundert*, Göttingen, 1983, II, pp. 490–513.
35. See the edition produced by Fausto Nicolini, 2 vols, Bari, 1916–29. The original edition is dated 1804–06; a wealth of information may be found in the bilingual edition, produced by Alain Pons and Michel Vovelle, of Cuoco's book, *Essai historique sur la révolution de Naples*, Belles Lettres, Paris, 2004.
36. See in particular pp. 17 (polemic against Bossuet), 44 and above all 172–87 (Atlantis). On the reception of the book, see B. Croce, *Storia della Storiografica italiana nel secolo decimonono*, I, Laterza, Bari, 1921, p. 56: 'Mazzoldi's book was generally received with respect and was discussed with gravity.'
37. William Blake, *The Complete Writings*, Keynes, London, 1958, p. 578 and 580. His relation to neo-Platonic philosophy is studied in an article by G.M. Harper, 'Blake's Neo-Platonic Interpretation of Plato's Atlantis Myth', *Journal of English and Germanic Philology* 59 (1955), pp. 72–9, which comments on the possible influence of Thomas Taylor's translation of the *Timaeus*, but not on the place of the myth in Blake's thought. On this subject, see K. Rayne, *Blake and Traditions*, 2 vols, London, 1969, who remarks: 'The Lost, Western Eden is sometimes America, sometimes Atlantis' (II, p. 268), but does not manage totally to elucidate the matter (ibid., pp. 423–9). I, for my part, will not venture to enter into details concerning these gnostic speculations.
38. *Complete Writings*, p. 649; see also p. 796: Adam himself was a Druid.

39. Ibid., pp. 637–8.
40. Ibid., p. 709.
41. It is worth remembering that he appears as the author of the *Ethiopica*, under 671 in Jacoby's *Corpus*.
42. F. Wilford, 'An essay on the 'Sacred Isles' in the West with Other Essays connected with that work', I, *Asiatic Researches* 8 (1805), see p. 247 (cited); Wilford also looked for Noah in the *Mahabharata* (see pp. 254–5); his study is to be found in subsequent volumes of *Asiatic Researches*, published in Calcutta. It is also reproduced in volumes 8–11 (1808–12) of the London edition of this important publication. My friend Charles Malamoud tells me that the çveta dvîpa are completely mythical islands and refers me to the remarks of W. Kirfel, *Die Kosmographie der Inder*, Bonn and Leipzig, 1920, pp. 18, 29, 30, 112.
43. *Atlantis in Ireland*, pp. 121, 327, 417, 505 and passim.
44. See his 'Essai sur les idées cosmographiques qui se rattachent au nom d'Atlas, considérées dans leur rapport avec les représentations antiques de ce personnage fabuleux', in *Bulletin universel*, VIIth section, XVII (1831), pp. 139–56.

Chapter 6

1. *Antiquités du département du Vaucluse*, Paris and Avignon, 1808, pp. 408–79.
2. Most of this information is provided by the nineteenth-century *Dictionnaire Larousse*.
3. *L'Atlantiade*, p. xix.
4. Ibid., p. 247.
5. *The Atlantic Syndrome*, Sutton Publishing, Sparkford, 2001. Atlantis according to Jules Verne is studied by Chantal Foucrier in her first publication, 'Jules Verne et l'Atlantide', *Nouvelles recherches sur Jules Verne et le voyage*, Paris, Minard, 1978, pp. 97–111.
6. In the Hachette edition, 1966, p. 102.
7. The Catalan text that I followed is that published by Father Farrès, Euma Editorial, Vic, 2002; I cite the trans. by A. Savine, Paris, 1883. *Les Atlantides imaginaires*, 2002, contains a study by Claude Lebigot on three Spanish authors, including Verdaguer, who refer to the myth of Atlantis.
8. Letter dated 18 July 1877, reproduced in the Farrès edition, p. 100.

9. Victor Bérard, *Les Navigations d'Ulysse, III, Calypso et la mer de l'Atlantide*, Paris, 1929; Adolf Schulten, 'Atlantis', *Rheinischer Museum für Philologie*, 88 (1939), pp. 326–46.

10. Dominique Alexandre Godron, *L'Atlantide et le Sahara*, part of a course of lectures to the Faculty of Sciences, Nancy University, in 1867; see C. Foucrier, *Le Mythe littéraire de l'Atlantide (1800–1939)*, p. 209.

11. See E.-F. Berlioux, 'Les Atlantes. Histoire de l'Atlantis et de l'Atlas primitif, ou Introduction à l'histoire de l'Europe', *Annuaire de la Faculté des Lettres de Lyon*, I, 1884, pp. 1–70.

12. *Auf dem Weg nach Atlantis*, Berlin, 1910. On the attempts of Leo Frobenius, see J. Imbelloni and A. Vivante, *Le Livre de l'Atlantide*, Paris, 1942, pp. 311–13.

13. Ministère de l'Instruction publique, *Exploration scientifique de la Tunisie. Géographie comparée de la province romaine d'Afrique* by Charles Tissot, former ambassador, member of the Institut, I, *Géographie physique. Géographie historique. Chorographie*, Imprimerie nationale, Paris, 1884, pp. 665–71.

14. P. Termier, 'L'Atlantide' (1913), *A la gloire de la Terre. Souvenirs d'un géologue*, Paris, 1922, pp. 131–2.

15. It has frequently been adapted for the cinema, in particular by Jacques Feyder (1921) and G.W. Pabst (1932), whose film Michel Desgranges kindly arranged for me to see.

16. *L'Enigme de l'Atlantide*, Paris, 2000, in the Blake and Mortimer series.

17. Aix-en-Provence, 1928; this little book followed an article, 'Le Mythe de l'Atlantide', *Mercure de France*, 15 Feb. 1927, pp. 29–71.

18. I am citing the edition of the novel published by Livre de Poche, with an introduction by Chantal Foucrier, p. 48.

19. See O. Boura, 'Une Faillite romanesque: l'Atlantide et le roman français dans la seconde moitié du xxe siècle', in the *Atlantides imaginaires* colloquium. On the other hand, the essay by Denis Saurat, *L'Atlantide et le règne des géants*, Paris, 1954, is inspired by Germanic interpretations.

20. Leipzig, 1931, vol. II of a tetralogy. In contrast, see the novel by Gerhart Hauptmann, *Atlantis*, Berlin, 1912, which C. Foucrier studies in her thesis.

21. *Atlantis die Urheimat der Arier mit eine Karte*, Arier-Verlag, Berlin, 1922, reprinted 1935.

22. Ibid., p. 94.

23. Berlin, 1934.

24. *Unsere Ahnen und Atlantis*, p. 25.

25. For example, Jean Deruelle, *L'Atlantide des mégalithes*, Paris, 1999, a book no more and no less raving than many others. See also Alberto Cesare Ambesi, *Atlantide, il Continente perduto*, Milan, 1994, in the occultist tradition, and Paul Dunbavin, *The Atlantis Researcher*, Nottingham, 1992, another author devoted to the culture of megaliths but who, perhaps out of British patriotism, believes Atlantis to lie in the Irish Sea, where it awaits underwater exploration.

26. On Homer and Plato, see *Unsere Ahnen*, pp. 144–53. The chapter is entitled 'Atlantis im Lichte Homers'.

27. I am citing the fourth edition, Munich, 1932, pp. 43–8.

28. See the fundamental book by M.H. Kater, *Das Ahnenerbe der S.S. 1933–1945. Ein Beitrag zur Kulturpolitik des Dritten Reiches*, Stuttgart, 1974; on Atlantis and Himmler, see pp. 51–71, 372, 378. A. Hermann was attached to this institute.

29. See P. Ory, *Le Petit Nazi illustré. 'Le Téméraire' (1943–1944)*, Paris, 1979, pp. 53–7. My colleague Axel Seeberg, of the University of Oslo, tells me that a similar comic strip was produced in occupied Norway, presumably on orders from Berlin.

30. See M.H. Kater, n. 28 above, p. 378, n. 109.

31. *Das enträtselte Atlantis*, Stuttgart, 1953 (French translation, Paris, 1964); *Atlantis, Heimat, Reich und Schicksal der Germanen*, Tübingen, 1965 (the publisher, Grabert, was openly Nazi); *Die Atlanter. Volk aus dem Bernsteinland*, Grabert, Tübingen, 1976.

32. This is clearly aimed at Otto Muck (1892–1956), the author of *Alles über Atlantis*, Dusseldorf and Vienna, 1976, French trans., *L'Atlantide. Légendes et réalités*, Paris, 1982.

33. *Die Atlanter*, pp. 416–24.

34. Thanks to Hélène Monsacré and Riccardo Di Donato, to whom I am most grateful.

35. Sergio Frau, *Le Colonne d'Ercole. Un Inchiesta come, quando e perchè la Frontiera di Herakles/Milqart, dio dell'Occidente, slittò per sempre a Gibilterra*, Rome, 2002.

36. That is to say between Tunisia and Sicily (not to be confused with the straits of Messina).

37. Frau, *Le Colonne d'Ercole*, pp. 416–76. The title of this section is

'Atlantide égale Scheria'. As I have shown above, I agree with this partial identification of Atlantis with the land of the Phaecians.

Chapter 7

1. In 'Entartete Musik' (Degenerate Music), p. 440, 854, 1994. It is thanks to Ingrid Galster that I possess this record. I learnt of the existence of the opera through the fine article by Timothée Picard, 'L'Atlantide et Auschwitz face à face: l'opéra *Der Kaiser von Atlantis* de V. Ullmann', in the *Atlantides imaginaires* collection; it was also through this friend that I discovered the book by Verena Naegele, *Victor Ullmann. Komponieren in verlorener Zeit*, Cologne, 2002.

2. Also performed in Paris in November 2004.

3. 'Auschwitz et l'Atlantide. Note sur un récit de Georges Perec'. The broad lines of my article were admirably developed by Robert Kahn, 'La trace du mythe, le mythe de la trace; W ou le souvenir d'enfance et l'Atlantide', in the Cérisy Colloquium collection, *Atlantides imaginaires*.

4. *Sigila*, no. 2 (October 1988), pp. 17–28.

5. 'Perec et la judéité', *Cahiers Georges Perec*, I, Paris, 1985, pp. 15–30.

6. *W*, respectively p. 57 and 10.

7. Ibid., p. 20.

8. Ibid., pp. 90–1.

9. Ibid., pp. 80–1.

10. Ibid., p. 213. Georges Perec, like many others, confuses the gas chambers with the crematorium furnaces where, as a general rule, only the dead went.

11. Ibid., pp. 116–21.

12. Ibid., pp. 179.

13. Ibid., pp. 205.

14. Ibid., pp. 218.

15. See Philippe Lejeune, *La Mémoire et l'oblique. Georges Perec autobiographe*, Paris, 1991.

16. Cited by P. Lejeune, ibid., p. 108.

17. See *The Black Hunter*, pp. 119–22.

Chapter 8

1. Respectively, *Psychanalyse du feu*, Gallimard, 1938; *L'Eau et les rêves. Essai sur l'imagination de la matière*, 1942; *L'Air et les Songes. Essai sur l'imagination du mouvement*, 1943; *La Terre et les rêveries de la volonté*, *La Terre et les rêveries du repos. Essai sur les images de l'intimité*, both published in 1948, the latter by José Corti).

2. *The Story of Atlantis. A Geographical, Historical, and Ethnological sketch*, London, 1896, 2nd edn, 1909; this book was regularly reprinted thereafter, for the last time, I believe, in 1970. It has been translated, certainly into French. On 'mystical' interpretations of this type, see the excellent chapter in Richard Ellis, *Imagining Atlantis*, New York, 1998, pp. 64–76.

3. I do not know why the title 'Madame' is systematically added to the name of this wife of a Russian general. The above-cited book by Paul Jordan, *The Atlantis Syndrome*, 2001, provides information about her, as do Chantal Foucrier's thesis and book.

4. Scott-Elliot is mentioned in, for example, the bibliography of the (at times scholarly) book by J. Imbelloni and A. Vivante, *Le Livre des Atlantides*, trans. into French by F. Gidon, Payot, 1942, and also, as a disciple of Madame Blavatsky's school, by Phyllis Young Forsyth, *Atlantis*, 1980, p. 7, mentioned above in Chapter 1; see also A.C. Ambesi, *Il Continente perduto*, Milan, 1994, in which the French translation is cited.

5. Colin Wilson and Rand Flem-Ath, *The Atlantis Blueprint. Unlocking the Ancient Mysteries of a Long-lost Civilization*, New York, 2000.

6. *Atlantis: the Antidiluvian World* is the title of the edition of this book, published in 1958, McLean, Virginia. The correct title of earlier editions is *The Antediluvian World*, New York, 1882. On Donnelly, see in particular E.S. Ramage (ed.), *Atlantis. Fact or Fiction?* (see the notes to the Introduction to that work, pp. 32–7); Richard Ellis, *Imagining Atlantis* (the same applies), pp. 38–42, and P. Jordan, *The Atlantis Syndrome* (the same applies), pp. 62–79, and the map on p. 67.

7. Jean Faure, *Champollion*, Fayard, 2004.

8. In Chapter 1, entitled 'The Purpose of the Book'.

9. Frank Joseph, *Atlantis in Wisconsin*, Lakeville, Minnesota, 1995. A covering note explains the connection with Donnelly. Frank Joseph's Atlantes come from the Canary Islands.

10. *Politics Ancient and Modern*, p. 57 and fig. 3; I refer to M.R. Stahl, *Atlantis Illustrated*, New York, 1982, which Alain Schnapp presented to me as a gift.

11. Nicoletta Salomon, *Venezia inabissata*, Mimesis collection, Milan, 2004.

Appendix

Two articles published on pages 10 and 11 of *The Times*, Friday 19 February 1909.*

THE LOST CONTINENT

(FROM A CORRESPONDENT)

The recent excavations in Crete have made it necessary to reconsider the whole scheme of Mediterranean history before the classical period.

Although many questions are still undecided, it has been established beyond any doubt that during the rule of the Eighteenth Dynasty in Egypt, when Thebes was at the height of its glory, Crete was the centre of a great empire whose trade and influence extended from the North Adriatic to Tell el Amarna and Africa was in Cretan hands, and the legends of Theseus seem to show that the Minoans dominated the Greek islands and the coasts of Attica.

This civilization was as ancient and as firmly established as it was wonderful. The beginning of the flint deposits found beneath the Palace at Knossos is considered by Dr Evans to date from at least 10,000 BC, and from that time onwards the development of the Minoan people can be traced continuously. Between the neolithic age and the final sack of Knossos three great periods can

---

* The anonymous author was the archaeologist K.T. Frost. I do not know who replied to him on behalf of *The Times*.

be distinguished which were roughly contemporary with the three great periods in Egypt—namely, the Memphite or Old Kingdom, the first Theban or Middle Kingdom, and the Eighteenth Dynasty or Theban Empire. During these periods there was close and constant communication between Crete and Egypt. A considerable trade was carried on between the two countries, which was accompanied by a certain exchange of influence and ideas.

On the other hand, the Minoan civilization was essentially Mediterranean, and is most sharply distinguished from any that arose in Egypt or the East. In some respects also it is strikingly modern. The many-storeyed palaces, some of the pottery, even the dresses of the ladies seem to belong to the modern rather than the ancient world. At the same time the number of Minoan sites and their extraordinary richness far exceed anything that Crete could be expected to produce, and must be due in part to that sea power which the ancient legends attributed to Minos.

Thus, when the Minoan power was at its greatest, its rulers must have seemed to the other nations to be mighty indeed, and their prestige must have been increased by the mystery of the lands over which they ruled (which seemed to Syrians and Egyptians to be the far West), and by their mastery over that element which the ancient world always held in awe. Strange stories, too, must have floated round the Levant of vast bewildering palaces, of sports and dances, and above all of the bullfight. The Minoan realm, therefore, was a vast and ancient power which was united by the same sea which divided it from other nations, so that it seemed to be a separate continent with a genius of its own.

Suddenly a swift and terrible destruction blotted out the Cretan power. Confident in their long supremacy at sea, the Minoans had left their cities unfortified, and the neglect of their land defences proved their ruin. The evidence is conclusive that some shock broke the sea power of Knossos when it was still full of vigour, still growing and developing; that a raid sacked the capital and desolated the island, and that thereafter the whole Minoan civilization decayed and finally vanished.

A new order of things arose; the Phoenicians took the place of the Minoans as traders and navigators, while on the coast of Greece and Asia Minor the Thalassocracies mentioned by Eusebius ruled in turn. It is true that Minoan influence lingered on in the art of the Aegean, but except for the legends of Minos, the very memory of the Minoans perished. As a political and commercial force, therefore, Knossos and its allied cities were swept away just when they seemed strongest and safest. It was as if the whole kingdom had sunk in the sea, as if the tale of Atlantis were true.

The parallel is not fortuitous. If the account of Atlantis is compared with the history of Crete and her relationship with Greece and Egypt, it seems almost certain that here we have an echo of the Minoans.

The story appears first in Plato. He says in the *Timaeus* that Solon went to Egypt and was told by a priest at Saïs (which was then the capital of Egypt) that in a bygone age there had been a great island State in the West which, in an attempt at universal conquest, made war on Greece and Egypt but was defeated by the Athenians and was overwhelmed by the sea, for its sins. Henceforth the place where the island had been was marked only by mudbanks, which were a danger to shipping. Solon would have been contemporary with the reign of Nocho II, exactly when Greek influence was strongest in the Delta, and when the two great camps at Daphnae and Naucratis were garrisoned by Greek mercenaries. The wisdom of the Egyptians had a fascination for the Greeks, and the conversation between Solon and the two priests, one of the most dramatic in all literature, may well have really taken place.

In many cases the whole description of Atlantis which is given in the *Timaeus* and the *Critias* has features so thoroughly Minoan that even Plato could not have invented so many unsuspected facts. He says of Atlantis: 'The island was the way to other islands, and from these islands you might pass to the whole of the opposite continent which surrounded the true ocean.' It is significant, too, that the empire is not described as a single homogeneous Power like Plato's republic and other States in fiction; on the contrary, it is a combination of different elements dominated by one city. 'In this island there was a great and wonderful empire which had rule over the whole island and several others, as well as over parts of the continent.' This sentence describes the political status of Knossos as concisely as the previous sentence describes the geographical position of Crete. Again, in the *Critias*, we read that the island was very lofty and precipitous on the side of the sea (as the Cretan coast generally is), but that the country immediately about and surrounding the city was a level plain sheltered from the North. This again corresponds exactly with the site of Knossos, which is on a low hill that rises from a plain and which is sheltered on the North by a protecting chain of hills. As Professor Burrows has observed, 'It was these hills that made its first stone-age citizen settle at Knossos at the nearest point up the Kairetos river that was safe from the eyes of the wandering pirate.' It is perhaps not too fanciful to connect the neolithic settlement with the 'earthborn' man Evenor, who was found by Poseidon on the site of the future city of Atlantis.

Further, the boundaries of the empire of Atlantis are identical with those assigned to Minoan influence. Atlantis is said to have ruled over North Africa as far as Egypt and over Europe as far as Tyrrhenia. Now, the connection between Tyrrhenia and Minoan Crete is in itself a most interesting problem. Pliny states on the authority of Varro that there were altogether four Labyrinths, and that the tomb of Lars Porsena of Clusium was one of them, the other three being at Knossos, Hawara, and Lemnos. In North Africa, too, the Turaha who settled near Gurob in the Fayum, and in whose graves 'Mycenean' pottery was found, seem to be the same as the Turasha who troubled Egypt in the reign of Morenptah.

The name thus falls into line with the group of names of invading tribes which can now almost certainly be equated with the Achaeans,

Teucri and Dana[o]i; that is to say with the nations associated with the later Kefts whom the Egyptians confused with the earlier Minoans. Although the legend of how Theseus slew the Minotaur with the help of the Cretan Princess whom he afterwards deserted is probably an echo of the raid that sacked Knossos, yet the facts and the date are still uncertain. It is quite certain, however, that men of Minoan race and appearance headed a great coalition of these people to conquer Egypt and rule the whole of the Eastern Mediterranean. This coalition was defeated by Rameses III, and his own account of the invasion can still be read on the walls of the Medinet Habu. The reliefs and inscriptions together place beyond doubt all the main features of this great fight on land and sea, the earliest known of the decisive battles of the world. Egypt was in the gravest danger, and was saved only by the splendid generalship of her king.

It is immaterial to the present argument whether the men whom Rameses defeated were true Minoans or whether they were the later Mycenaeans, for the Egyptians themselves hopelessly confused the two peoples. The central fact remains that men whom the Egyptians considered Minoans did head a confederacy of nations and did aspire to what seemed universal conquest; and, although this attack was defeated by the Egyptians, yet the legends indicate that Knossos itself was overthrown by the pre-Dorian inhabitants of Greece proper, who were represented in Solon's time by the Athenians.

An obvious difficulty in identifying Crete with Atlantis is that Crete is inside the Pillars of Hercules, whereas Atlantis is stated most expressly to have been outside them. Although this objection seems formidable, the confusion can be shown to have arisen in a perfectly natural manner, if we imagine ourselves at Saïs and take the same geographical point of view as the Egyptian priests. It is the name which has caused the difficulty, and we are expressly told that the names in the story had been translated into Egyptian and were given Greek equivalents by Solon. The Egyptian version probably said 'an island in the furthest west'. Crete, an island in the open sea, would indeed have seemed in the furthest west to the coast-hugging mariners of the Memphito or even the Theban kingdom. It was probably the only voyage they made in which they lost sight of land. But in Solon's time the geographical horizon had widened, and the Phoenicians had long been accustomed to trade with Spain. He was even contemporary with their circumnavigation of Africa in the service of the king of Egypt. Romance, therefore, must be sought further west, out in the real ocean beyond the Pillars of Hercules. Possibly here we have an echo of an Egyptian phrase which said beyond the Four Pillars of the World, which Crete would have been according to early Egyptian reckoning, for at first the Four Pillars were identified with actual mountains.

But a stronger argument is furnished by the strange and persistent tradition of the shallowness of the Atlantic Ocean and the mud-banks which marked the place where Atlantis had been. We cannot imagine that the first navigators who sailed west of Gibraltar brought back tales of the shallowness of those seas; on the contrary they must have been impressed with their depth, vastness and the absence of islands. But if Atlantis were Crete the explanation is easy, for if through bad weather or faulty reckoning a ship were to miss Crete and pass it on the south, it would soon find itself on the quicksands off the Tunisian coast, the Syrtes which were dreaded even in Roman times. After the Minoan power had been swept away in perhaps little more than the 'day and a night' given by legend it would be easy to consider that these shoals were the remains of the island kingdom that had been engulfed in the sea by the gods.

In broad outlines, therefore, the history and geography of Minoan Crete correspond exactly with what Plato tells us of Atlantis; but the similarity in detail is no less striking. The great harbour, for example, with its shipping and its merchants coming from all parts, the elaborate bath rooms, the stadium, and the solemn sacrifice of a bull are all thoroughly, though not exclusively, Minoan; but when we read how the bull is hunted 'in the temple of Poseidon without weapons but with staves and nooses' we have an unmistakable description of the bull-ring at Knossos, the very thing which struck foreigners most and which gave rise to the legend of the Minotaur. Plato's words exactly describe the scenes on the famous Vaphio cups which certainly represent catching wild bulls for the Minoan bull-fight, which, as we know from the palace itself, differed from all others which the world has seen in exactly the point which Plato emphasizes—namely, that no weapons were used.

It seems therefore that Solon really did hear a tale in Saïs which filled him with wonder and which was really the true but misunderstood Egyptian record of the Minoans, though neither Solon nor the Priest dreamed of identifying the sea-girt empire of tradition with Crete, the little island which had loomed so large to their forefathers.

But at the time when Knossos was sacked, the sudden destruction of the ruler of the seas and the chief commercial power of the Levant would in some degree have resembled the sack of London today. An event which concerned the Egyptians so closely must have been entered in their annals, and once written in them the account would have been faithfully transcribed whether understood or not. Here we have a curious sidelight: Proclus asserts that he saw pictures of Atlantis in Egypt, and that there were many such in the country. If he means Kefts or Minoans his words are intelligible, for they are represented in some of the most striking reliefs that still remain in Egypt.

Thus there is a historical basis for Plato's legend, as in the case of Gyges. But Plato himself professes to have taken his story not from Egypt but from the poem which Solon contemplated. Hence the Athenian State, which in its idealized form is fictitious. For Solon seems to have conceived the idea of an epic in which all the non-Hellenic nations of the world should rally round Atlantis in a struggle against Hellas, of which Athens was the champion. To ensure poetic unity he would omit the attack on Egypt by Atlantis and would even use the wonders of Egypt and Babylon to embellish his island empire: his poem should be as much greater than 'the tale of Troy divine' as Minos was greater than Priam. The *Critias* probably represents the beginning of the poem which because of his political labours was never finished. Critias probably really had the original manuscript of Solon, as Plato states, and for this reason his name was given to the unfinished dialogue. The greatness of the theme, the romance of its inception, the dramatic irony and the strange chances of the preservation of this epic are unequalled in all literature.

The much wider question of the co-relation of the great movements of the Mediterranean peoples at this period has already been dealt with by Professor Currelly, of Toronto. Here it is sought to demonstrate that the long-lost Atlantis is neither more nor less than Minoan Crete.

ATLANTIS

Ever since Plato left half-told in the *Timaeus* and the *Critias* the story of Atlantis, the great island kingdom in the Western Ocean beyond the Pillars of Hercules, geographers and other commentators have exercised themselves in vain to give a local habitation to the now submerged kingdom and to identify it with some known region of the habitable globe. 'As many attempts', says Jowett, 'have been made to find the great island as to discover the country of the lost tribes. Interpreters have looked for the spot in every part of the globe, America, Palestine, Arabia, Felix, Ceylon, Sardinia, Sweden'. The story—Jowett calls it a fiction, but we will not here beg the question—has also 'exercised a great influence over the imagination of later ages'. It is the prototype, or the parent in various degrees of propinquity of the 'Vera Historia' of Lucian, and possibly of the late Greek fable of Syntipas—though that is said to be derived from a Persian source, and may have some obscure connection with the travels of Sinbad the Sailor and other narratives in the Arabian Nights—and of all those apologues or fables in which medieval or modern writers have essayed to enshrine their own ideas or to satirize the foibles of existing States. Of this large family, to mention only a few, are the fantastic imaginings in this kind of Rabelais, More's 'Utopia', Bacon's 'New Atlantis', 'Gulliver's Travels', Voltaire's 'Micromegas' and many less famous apologues. In another direction, associated or confused with the independent legend of the Hesperides, Plato's Atlantis has given rise to—or, perhaps, having regard to what is now known concerning the migration of fables along independent lines from a common prehistoric source, we should rather say is collateral with—a whole range of mythological fancy concerning certain fabled Islands of the Blest, which has taken various forms, all marked by a strong family likeness, among nearly all the maritime races of Europe. Is there any foundation in fact for this fascinating and widespread story? That is the question once more raised by the ingenious speculation concerning 'The Lost Continent', which we print elsewhere, from the pen of a Correspondent, who finds in the explorations recently conducted with such astonishing results by Dr Arthur Evans on the site of Knossos in Crete a solid foundation in fact for what might otherwise be regarded more as the creation of Plato's abounding fancy.

We must leave our Correspondent's arguments and speculations to speak for themselves, merely offering them without prejudice the friendly hospitality of our columns. Of course, if Plato's story can be assumed to have any foundations in fact at all, the traditions of the great Minoan kingdom in Crete, still surviving in his time, might in the light of recent discoveries very well be represented as having furnished that foundation. Many of the statements of Herodotus, which by earlier generations of critics were dismissed as mere travellers' tales, have, in the light of modern archaeological research, been fully established as solid historical facts; and in general it may be said that a good deal of the destructive 'higher criticism' which once found favour with scholars has now been disallowed by the archaeologists. But Herodotus, after all, was a professed historian, credulous it may be, and not without a certain mythopoeic tendency of his own—even Thucydides has been represented by a modern scholar [F.M. Cornford] as 'mythistoricus'—but nevertheless a diligent searcher after truth. Plato, on the other hand, was no professional historian, nor did he pretend to restrict his abounding fancy within the limits of historical fact. 'My dear Socrates,' he made Phaedrus say, in the dialogue of that name, 'We all know how easy it is for you to place your stories in Egypt, or anywhere else you please.' In the *Timaeus*, after listening to the beginning of the story of Critias about Atlantis, Socrates says of it—surely not without a sly touch of his well-known irony—that 'it has the very great advantage of being a fact and not a fiction'. Plato was a consummate master of the art of investing his most daring fancies with the solid seeming of established fact. Critias, who is made to tell the story, certainly tells it in the best Platonic manner. He took a night to think it over and to refresh his memory of what he heard in his callow boyhood from his grandfather, also named Critias, a man of ninety years at the time. Critias the elder was the son of Dropidas, a relative and intimate friend of Solon, who often recited to Dropidas the unfinished poem in which he had enshrined the story of Atlantis, its widespread dominions, and its sudden extinction when the gods grew angry with it, as he had heard from the priests of Saïs, in the Egyptian Delta. No doubt Solon in his narrative to Dropidas completed the story, which Plato and Critias left half told, in plain, unvarnished prose. As for the alleged poem, there is, says Jowett, no other trace of it in antiquity, so that all the documentary evidence we have for the Egyptian origin of the story or for any vestige of actual fact in it, is the version of it put by Plato into the mouth of Critias in the two dialogues already mentioned. As to the Egyptian origin assigned to it by Plato, that is easily explained. 'You Greeks', he makes the priests of Saïs say to Solon, 'are merely children, and you have no sense or knowledge of real antiquity. You have not even a tradition of the greatest achievement of your race when the Athenians single-handed withstood the power of Atlantis. The reason is that in the days following your great victory over Atlantis, Attica was visited by a great convulsion of nature which spared only the illiterate dwellers in the hill-country and wiped out all the records of your past. In that same convulsion Atlantis disappeared altogether, sinking beneath the sea. We Egyptians, however, are happily exempt from these convulsions of nature and our records of the times which have been forgotten are continuous and complete. We can tell you all about Atlantis and its divine origin, its wondrous power, its widespread dominions, the marvels of its city and its surroundings. We can also tell you how the Athenians alone set a boundary to its aggressions, and why, when it grew degenerate, the anger of the gods doomed it to destruction and the very seat of its power sank for ever beneath the waves.' But that is the unfinished part of the story which Plato and Critias left half told.

The above is merely a bald and abridged paraphrase of Plato's inimitable narrative. Does it wear the aspect of historical verisimilitude, apart from traditions of Minoan supremacy which undoubtedly survived in Plato's day, and may very well explain the coincidences on which our Correspondent insists between the story of Atlantis and the results of the explorations at Knossos? 'No one', says Jowett, 'knew better than Plato how to invent a noble lie.' His object plainly was to glorify Athens and find in an imagined and wholly forgotten antiquity prehistoric precedent for the progress of Athens during the Persian Wars. All the Greeks were impressed with the immemorial antiquity of Egypt and could not but contrast it with the short and troubled annals of their own recent emergence from the unknown past. Hence, when Plato wanted to get beyond the narrow bounds of time and space that limited his own historical outlook, to what better source could he go than to the Egypt of his own imagination, and how could he better give authority to his dream than by pretending to take it from the lips of the much-travelled and much-troubled legislator whom all Athenians justly honoured as one of the seven sages of Greece? 'Plato here, as elsewhere', says Jowett, 'ingeniously gives the impression that he is telling the truth which mythology had corrupted, and probably he never dreamed that posterity would take him literally. Yet the world, like a child, has readily, and for the most part unhesitatingly, accepted the tale of the Island of Atlantis. In modern times we hardly seek for traces of the submerged continent: but even Mr Grote is inclined to believe in the Egyptian poem of Solon, of which there is no evidence in antiquity.' Even if Plato's story was an invention, however, we need not assume that it was a pure creation of his fancy. He might work into it anything that he had heard or read of earlier civilizations and dominions existing within the circuit of the Hellenic world. On that hypothesis the correspondences noted by our Correspondent between the story of Atlantis and the revelations of Knossos may very well engage the serious attention of scholars and archaeologists.

INDEX OF PROPER NAMES